"Many critics focus on God's actions in prove Christianity. Dr. Kaiser's efforts show the inaccuracy of this approach, offering a compelling look at how God's work in the past is consistent with the teachings of the New Testament. This important method will better equip leaders at all levels of the faith."

—Dr. John Ankerberg, president and host of *The John Ankerberg Show*

"In *Tough Questions about God and His Actions in the Old Testament*, Dr. Kaiser skillfully mingles biblical brilliance and conversational applicability. Few can do both well, especially tackling the more problematic issues found in the Old Testament. This book is just one more addition to his canon of publications that will benefit the ministry of leaders and the life of thoughtful Christians. Having known Dr. Kaiser as a colleague and as a friend for over twenty years, I know that what he writes he believes, and what he believes he lives. Anyone who desires to know God's Word more deeply and believe it more convincingly should read this book."

—Barry H. Corey, President, Biola University

"For several millennia certain passages in the Old Testament have perplexed careful readers of the Scriptures. Dr. Kaiser, with his customary exegetical and theological acumen, gets to the heart of these perplexing passages by wonderfully explaining and shedding insightful light on these difficult texts. This is an opportune resource—arriving amid increasingly complex times—for Christians who desire to explain God and his ways. Consequently, this book equips students of the Scriptures to better understand and teach the full extent of God's word, without apology but with clarity and full confidence in the character, words, and plan of our triune God."

—Dorington Little, Senior Pastor, First Congregational Church, Hamilton, MA

Tough Questions about God and His Actions in the Old Testament

Walter C. Kaiser Jr.

Kregel
Publications

Published by Kregel Publications, a division of Kregel, Inc., 2450 Oak Industrial Dr. NE, Grand Rapids, MI 49505-6020.

ISBN 978-0-8254-4376-3

Printed in the United States of America
15 16 17 18 19 / 5 4 3 2 1

Dedicated to
Mrs. Susie Rowan,
Executive Director of
Bible Study Fellowship International

Contents

Introduction

Question:
How shall we answer tough questions about God and His actions in the Old Testament?

Much of the current antipathy to the Old Testament seems to have begun as early as the middle of the second Christian century with a ship owner named Marcion who died around 154 AD. He was the son of a Christian bishop but, for the first time in the faith's early history, dissociated the two testaments of the Bible, preferring the New Testament over against the Old Testament. Even though the church ultimately rejected Marcion's bold (but futile) attempt to demean the Old Testament, if not to get rid it and to replace it with most of the New Testament, there still lingers in Christian thought today the haunting suspicion that there may indeed be a difference between the two testaments. It is to this suspicion that this book is addressed.

The first use of the expression "Old Testament," as applied to the first thirty-nine books of the Bible, didn't appear until much later in the fourth century AD in the writings of Eusebius of Caesarea. Clearly, Eusebius started this divisive reference with the distinct intention to show the superiority of the New Testament over the Old Testament—even though the New Testament proclaims that "all Scripture is inspired by God" (2 Tim. 3:16).

Centuries later, G. L. Bauer (1755–1806) wrote the first book to use the title *Old Testament Theology* (1796), wherein he tried to show that the Old and New Testaments belonged to two different inspirations and that the Old Testament was foreign to the Christian faith. The outcry for the removal of the Old Testament from the canon of Scripture grew louder by the time of Adolf von Harnack (1851–1930). Harnack denounced the practice of retaining the Old Testament as part of the Christian canon as "an ecclesiastical and religious paralysis." Friedrich Delitzsch (1850–1922)[1] wrote *Die Grosse Tauschung* (*The Great Deception)* in 1920, in which he argued that the Old Testament was not a Christian book and the New Testament superseded it. Even more recently, Rudolf Bultmann (1884–1976) adopted explicit Marcionite views as he advocated that the Old Testament was a witness to a miscarriage of history as Israel failed to obey the law, which therefore necessitated the need for grace to replace it. The Old Testament was not a document for Christian faith according to Bultmann. Even Karl Barth (1886–1968), who did not agree with Bultmann, still usually stayed away from the Old Testament as he unadvisedly opposed the New Testament God of grace to the Old Testament God of law.

Marcion is also credited with beginning what became a Christian overemphasis on salvation over against creation. Marcion made the God of the Old Testament the exclusive Demiurge, the Creator, who was different from the Savior of the world. Thus, as some have correctly pointed out, Christians tended to fix their attention almost exclusively on God's deliverance of Israel from Egypt, rather than joining this theme with the theme of creation. As a result, all too often, nature and the physical world had no interest for the Christian community. Christians all too frequently tended to think only of themselves and their own salvation in a much too narrow way. Accordingly, the physical world and the human body were replaced mainly by a spiritual view of deliverance in Christ alone. The realm of the spirit tended to swallow up all attention to the physical or material world.

Therefore, as negative statements concerning the first testament grew within the scholarly community, a large number of questions were raised about the first thirty-nine books of the Bible. Unfortunately, they were all too often left unanswered, which seemed to be reason enough to downgrade the significance and importance of the first testament.

This is why we feel that it is time that issues regarding the Old Testament were faced as straightforwardly as possible. This challenge is especially relevant for those in their upper teens and in college or graduate school—the twenty- and thirty-somethings! They compromise the largest segment of a new group of "Nons"—the non-attenders at church and the non-religious. Discussion questions are included in each chapter that will hopefully engage readers in a deeper consideration of these issues. This is not to leave middle-aged or senior folks out of the picture, for oftentimes their questions are just as challenging as any that

---

1.   Not to be confused with his godly father, Franz Delitzsch (1813–1890).

younger generations are asking. So this book might often be best read in small study groups in homes where the focus is on one chapter or portion of Scriptures at a time. But neither would it be unthinkable for a pastor to choose to do a series of messages on these chapters that would bring new health to the body of Christ and then to follow those sermons up with a discussion time. It would be a time of great growth for the body of Christ.

The need to understand the proper role of the Old Testament in Christian thinking and experience and for understanding the ways that God as depicted in the Old Testament has recently assumed a much larger role in our society with the rise of the New Atheism and, as we have already alluded to another group, the increasing number of dropouts from the church in the twenty-to-thirty-year-old range. A great number of questions have arisen that could be called "tough questions about God and his actions in the Old Testament," especially as they relate to today's world. It seems as if all too often God is depicted by readers of the Old Testament as someone whose character appears to be less loving and gracious than the way the New Testament seems to present his character.

Could this be an accurate portrayal of the same God who was revealed in our Lord Jesus Christ? Why is it that the teaching ministries of the church and Bible study groups appear to focus mainly on the second person of the Trinity by urging that all sermons and teachings in our day ought to be "Christocentric" and "Redemptive-Historical"? Is this a deliberate attempt to avoid these issues as if they have no solution? Jesus indeed is central to the message of the Bible, but we must never indulge in a Christo-*exclusivism* that downplays the rest of the teaching of the Bible.

There is only one way to decide on how to answer this critique of the Old Testament and the questions that most do not seem to want to talk about: we must take up the most challenging issues that seem to cast the longest shadow on God's character and his actions in the past in order to see if such depictions are accurate and truly represent who God is and what he has done! Therefore, this book proposes to openly and honestly face these charges and to answer them with valid responses from the same biblical texts that are the basis for these challenges.

Some readers of Scripture approach the Old Testament with a sympathetic attitude, recognizing that while there are indeed a host of issues in this portion of Scripture, it is nonetheless God's Word. Other readers, however, focus on a list of problems that form a series of great stumbling blocks to their appreciation of parts or even the entirety of the Old Testament. For example, here are just two of the offsetting issues directly from Old Testament materials that are puzzling to say the least:

> Uzzah reached out instinctively to save the Ark of the Covenant when stumbling oxen endangered the ark of God, but who was nevertheless struck dead for doing so (2 Sam. 6:6–9).

> Forty-two children were mauled by two bears for mocking the prophet Elisha (2 Kings 2:23–25).[2]

These, and more, are often given as evidence that the God of the Old Testament is rather heavy-handed, swift to judgment, and beyond our ability to understand at times. At least he does not seem to possess the same type of love and grace that Jesus exudes in the New Testament. In that testament, God is presented as the person from whom all goodness, kindness, and grace flows. In the Old Testament, however (it is claimed), God is presented as possessing a mixture of anger and love, judgment and grace. How are we to explain this combination? Is God shown altogether differently in the New Testament presentation?

This distorted picture presents such a contrast that it is certainly a different picture from the one actually found in the Old Testament context itself. Some of the reasons for such an unbalanced view can be attributed to the fact that many who read the Bible read the New Testament much more frequently than they do the Old Testament. Therefore, their understanding of the Old Testament context is often marginal and episodic compared to their understanding of the New. Others complain about the antiquity of the Old Testament. They say that its culture is too far removed from ours for us to sense its relevance. Others point to the fact that many of its books are too long for readers to capture the overall thrust and central meaning of individual books and how each contributes to the total meaning of the Old Testament.

Regardless of which explanation above best explains why many have bypassed the Old Testament or found it to be beyond their understanding, the reality is that the Old Testament contains over three-fourths of the revelation God has communicated to us. To avoid reading it is to miss the *majority* of what

---

2. Since every difficult passage of the Old Testament cannot be discussed in the present book, please see the explanation given to the two citations listed above in *Hard Sayings of the Bible* by Walter C. Kaiser, Jr. et al. (Downers Grove, IL: IVP, 1996), 219–221, 232–34.

God has given us for our edification and insight. Can Christians dare refuse to listen to this disclosure of the mind of God and of his preparation for the person and work of his Son? To the extent that we selectively read and study the Bible, especially the Old Testament, we develop a type of biblical illiteracy and therefore remained unformed and untaught in portions of Christian truth.

There is another group of Old Testament users who do interact with the Old Testament, but they do so in such a way that they allow the New Testament to get in the way of actually understanding what the Old Testament has to say. These readers take a later rendering of an Old Testament passage in the New Testament in such a contorted way that the reader incorrectly re-interprets the Old Testament from the New Testament perspective, which the reader then accepts as the authoritative and exclusive meaning on that Old Testament text. To go *first* to the New Testament interpretation as the source for the original and final meaning of an Old Testament text, reading that alleged New Testament meaning back into the Old Testament, is methodologically flawed and wrongheaded. In effect, it makes the Old Testament meaning dispensable and reduces it to mean the same thing as the most recent application of that text in the New Testament. This levels out the whole of the Bible to always say what it said in its latest and most recent communication of the divine meaning, which at the very least is reductionistic and, at its worst, destructive of meaning in Scripture.

This is not to deny that the New Testament writers have a legitimate freedom in interpreting the Old Testament according to the author's intentions and then applying that biblical text to related areas. Such a procedure, however, should never be used as a shortcut for interpreters to understanding the point of view and claims of the Old Testament author or as the first order of business in trying to understand an Old Testament text.

One of the most important principles of interpretation is that we should allow the biblical writer to say first of all what he wanted to say before we apply that truth or even ask how, in the progress of revelation, that truth was supplemented and advanced in the whole canon by New Testament comments on that same text.

We can also add to this list of issues, the outcries of the New Atheists who are not hesitant to pile up a long list of charges against the Old Testament. Some of these will be listed in our first chapter. Are the charges that have been raised from Marcion to the interpreters and critics of the present day unfairly leveled? Would our Lord really dispose of three-fourths of the revelation he has given to us? It is this author's conviction that the Old Testament can once again be upheld as the distinctive revelation of God. Moreover, God's character, actions, and teachings during that same time period carried with them His own time-limits, authority, and principles for later application within its body of truth. God's name, character, reputation, works, and purposes were beautiful, righteous, just, fair and upright. It is with this purpose, then, that we propose to tackle these tough questions.

1

The God of Mercy or the God of Wrath?

Question: *Is the God of the Old Testament a God of love and mercy or a God of wrath and judgment?*

The contemporary neo-atheist Richard Dawkins, in his best-selling book *The God Delusion,* wrote these stinging words about the God of the Old Testament:

> The God of the Old Testament is arguably the most unpleasant character in all fiction: jealous and proud of it; a petty, unjust, unforgiving control-freak; a vindictive, bloodthirsty ethnic cleanser; a misogynistic, homophobic, racist, infanticidal, genocidal, filicidal, pestilential, megalomaniacal, sadomasochistic, capriciously malevolent bully.[1]

What is amazing is not only the bitterness that runs like acid through the course of his words, but the fact that his book has become an international best-seller. Does this huge number of sales in the Western world indicate that from a global perspective those who live in what used to be regarded as the Christian West have concluded that the God of the Old Testament is different from the Jesus of the New Testament?

---

1. Richard Dawkins. *The God Delusion* (New York, NY: Mariner, 2008), 51.

Previously, in 2007, another neo-atheist, Christopher Hitchens, published a similar best-seller entitled *God Is Not Great: How Religion Poisons Everything*.[2] Hitchens (recently deceased) had the same anti-God sentiments, which he set forth just as provocatively as did Dawkins. It seemed as if the negative view of God, especially as he was depicted in the Old Testament, was becoming the flavor of the new decade that introduced the twenty-first century. Did this also mean that a new majority of persons now agreed with these neo-atheists, despite the extremely acerbic nature of such bitter characterizations of the living God?

Dawkins's attacks, in particular, were focused on the Old Testament God for he also wrote another article entitled "Atheists for Jesus"[3] (an apparent take-off on the name "Jews for Jesus"). In that piece, he even allowed that "Jesus is a huge improvement over the cruel ogre of the Old Testament."[4] But this was a small consolation, given how vitriolic his attacks on God in the older testament were.

The basis for such charges against God are usually anchored in poor readings and interpretations of various difficult passages in the Old Testament. If there was a way to dramatize or misread what the Bible taught in the Old Testament, then that meaning was immediately adopted and exalted as another mark against the respectable character of God.

A second fault that could be detected in these negative views of God and his character was that they absolutely detested any statement about God's judgment, wrath, or anger against evil, wrong, sin, or unrighteousness. Instead, they focused on the quality of God's love, which was often exalted in some of these writers, to a point where God became a being simply and totally characterized by an all-consuming love with no evidence of his disapproval of evil or his dislike or hatred of sin, injustice or any evil.

The Anger and Wrath of God

It was a heretic named Marcion, who (despite the fact that his father was a pastor) brought the issue of God's anger to a head as early as AD 140. But the Hebrew word for "anger" (*'ap*, meaning "nose," because anger is seen first in the face) goes back pretty far in time, especially to the story of the Exodus. There "anger" is used ten times of God and Moses (Exod. 4:14; 11:8; 15:8; 22:24;

2. Christopher Hitchens. *God is Not Great: How Religion Poisons Everything* (New York, NY: Hatchette Book Group, 2007).
3. Richard Dawkins, "Atheists for Jesus," *Free Inquiry* 25 (2005): 9–10.
4. Dawkins, *The God Delusion*, 283.

32:10, 11, 12, 19, 22; 34:6). These texts need now to be sampled to test the challenges brought against them by the New Atheists.

Moses was called by God to lead Israel out of Egypt, but Moses objected four times. Each time God countered Moses objections with divine assurance of assistance. Moses finally objected a fifth time, without any kind of good or clear reason, but with a simple refusal that he would not accept God's call to lead his people Israel out of Egypt. This excited the anger of God! Later, Moses himself also got angry with an intransigent and unrelenting Pharaoh (11:8), but it is the anger of God that dominated this narrative of the Exodus, and that is what attracted the ire of some, such as the noted neo-atheists in our day.

It is also important to note right from the get-go that this same text that emphasizes the wrath of God is the same text where God is also said to be "slow to anger" (literally, "long-nosed"). This description of God occurs frequently throughout the Old Testament, including Exodus 34:6, Numbers 14:18; Nehemiah 9:17; Psalms 86:15; 103:8; 145:8; Joel 2:13; Jonah 4:2; and Nahum 1:3. In fact, this was so much a part of Yahweh's nature, that he dramatically announced this feature as part of his name in Exodus 34:6–7. There God passed by in front of Moses, proclaiming, "Yahweh, Yahweh, the compassionate and gracious God, slow to anger, abounding in love and faithfulness, maintaining love to thousands, and forgiving wickedness, rebellion, and sin" (my translation).

Thus God pointed out the essence of his compassion, his slowness to anger and his love and grace. This grace of God and his slowness to anger was announced at the very same time that Yahweh had become furious with his people for setting up and worshiping the golden calf (Exod. 32:10). Nevertheless, God still abounded in forgiveness and love, despite all of these acts of disloyalty; he was full of "love and kindness" (Hebrew, "full of *hesed* and *emet*, "full of grace and truth") to sinning Israel. That is the topic that must be explored more fully if we are to understand who this God actually is.

The Loving Kindness/Grace of God in the Old Testament

There is a special term for one of God's most celebrated characteristics taken from Exodus 34:6–7. It is the Hebrew word *hesed*, which occurs about 250 times in the Old Testament, yet it is by far the most difficult word for which to find a precise equivalent English word(s) to translate it since no one, two, or more English equivalents fully capture all that is intended in this Hebrew word. It is variously rendered as "loving-kindness," "covenantal love," "mercy," or perhaps it is best rendered simply by our word: "grace."

This word is used most frequently in the Psalms (123 times), but even there it is used most often of all to describe Yahweh's character. His "loving kindness" or "grace" is enormously bountiful, yet it is simultaneously steadfast and dependable. It is the overwhelming love and grace from God to those who least deserved it, but, in God's tenderness, he has reached out to his sinful people and showed them his grace. Yes, the Lord does get angry, but he never flies off the handle abruptly nor does he lose his temper as mortals do. Instead, God is slow and deliberate in the practice of his anger, always more than willing to extend his grace and love. God has no desire whatsoever to even the score or to remain implacable. He has no potential rivals with whom he sees himself in competition with or wanting to get level with them on their plane.

It is only when anger and wrath, as practiced among humans more often than not, are left unchecked and uncontrolled in mortals that such anger becomes an evil that must be faced and dealt with. But God's anger is never explosive, unreasonable, irrational, or one that is out of control. Rather it is an anger that is controlled in God, which he uses as an instrument of his will, without at the same time shutting off his mercy, grace, and compassion to the same sinners (Ps. 77:9). Moreover, his anger marks the end of any perceived indifference on his part to evil, for it is impossible for him to remain neutral or impartial in the presence of evil (Isa. 26:20; 54:7–8; 57:16–19). Yahweh's love remains despite Israel's disobedience and even in spite of our own rebellion (Jer. 31:3; Hos. 2:19), which is almost inconceivable.

Along with this important word for "grace" in the Old Testament is the Hebrew verb "to love" (Hebrew, *'ahab*), which occurs in the Old Testament thirty-two times, twenty-three of which describe God's love for Israel or for particular individuals. In addition to this, the noun form of this word for "love" appears another four times, making a total of twenty-seven times that God's love for humans is affirmed in the Old Testament.

In an attempt to define the love of God, C. S. Lewis gave us four possible analogies for this love of God, but it was his fourth analogy, the love that exists between a husband and his wife, that helps us to best approximate the love of God. In one of Lewis' finest statements, he concluded, this love between a husband and his wife is a love wherein each is willing "to forgive the most" (because love is willing to look beyond and live with any perceived faults) while at the same time "it condones the least" (because that love, while continuing to love, nevertheless does not cease coaxing, urging, and hoping for the best in the other partner). In the same way, God continues to forgive graciously, while he simultaneously maintains his high and holy standard for all that is good, right, and just, in each person. It is precisely this very same tension between forgiving the most, yet condoning the least, that can begin to help explain God's love for us.

However, this still leaves the question not faced as yet as to how we can reconcile the anger of God with the love of God. In the history of the church, this became the question of divine passibility (i.e., whether God was capable of having feelings or emotions of any sort) over against divine impassibility (i.e., whether God was without a capacity to feel, suffer, or be angry at anything). Gnosticism took a strong lead in this discussion and denied that God could indeed experience anger, suffering, or any other feelings. Marcion, the second-century heretic, as already mentioned, also declared that God was free of all such affections or feelings and therefore was impassible.

It was the church father Lactantius, who in the later part of the third century AD, put the question in a more biblical perspective. He argued: "He who loves the good also hates the evil, and he who does not hate the evil does not love the good because, on the one hand, to love the good comes from hatred of evil and to hate evil rises *from the love of the good.*"[5]

Our modern difficulty in accepting that anger can be a part of the character of God is related to our improper and incorrect association of anger with "the desire for retaliation" or "the desire to get even," as Aristotle[6] and others taught. But anger, properly defined, is the legitimate emotion of a person rising to resist evil, not an attempt to get even or to right what we felt was a wrong in a way that put us, as the objectors, on a higher plane than those we accused. Therefore, anger does not need to be explosive, unchecked, or something out of control. In fact, God's anger, the Scriptures teach, passes quickly (Isa. 26:20; 54:7–8; 57:16–19), lasting but for a moment while God's love endures forever (Jer. 31:31; Hos. 2:19).

If it is true that God has both a soft side and a hard side in the exercise of his love and his anger, how does God himself relate these two sides, especially in the Old Testament? One of the classic passages in the Old Testament where Yahweh expresses his own tension between his anger and his compassion is found in Ho-

5. Lactantius, *The Minor Works: De ira Dei [The Wrath of God]*. Trans. Sister Mary Francis Mc-Donald (Washington, DC: Catholic University of American Press, 1965), 154:69.

6. Aristotle, *De Anima*, 1:1. See the excellent discussion on this whole topic by Abraham Heschel, *The Prophets* (New York: Harper & Row, 1962), 2:1–86, especially 60n4.

sea 11:8–9. Certainly Israel needed to be reproved for she had gone off on her own way and sinned grievously, yet she was addressed as Yahweh's "son" (Hos. 11:1), and the thought of "overthrowing" or "hand[ing her] over" to judgment (Hos. 11:8) so aroused God's "compassion" that it made him almost like someone who was about to vomit or throw up. The passage says:

> How can I give you up, Ephraim? How can I hand you over, Israel? How can I treat you like Admah? How can I make you like Zeboyim? My heart is changed within me; all my compassion is aroused. I will not carry out my fierce anger, nor will I devastate Ephraim again. For I am God, and not man—the Holy One among you.

The reason why God cannot carry out what ordinarily he might do in a case like this is because he is God and not a mortal being like other men (Hos. 11:9). God is the Holy One, therefore his actions must show him to be separate and different from those responses that might come from mere mortals. Admah and Zeboyim were two of the five cities of the plain that were destroyed when Lot was told to leave Sodom and Gomorrah before God's judgment struck. It is texts such as these that make it difficult to argue that the God of the Old Testament is some sort of harsh and unfeeling despot. The reality that God needed to punish his people is seen as emotionally wrenching. Despite what Israel deserved. God's compassion would not allow it to take place. He showed enormous reticence to execute anger so that love and grace were in the forefront.

For some, however, the most notorious example of Yahweh's alleged hatefulness, some argue, is found in the line, "Jacob I loved, but Esau I hated" (Mal. 1:2–3; Rom. 9:13). But how could a deity claim to still love a person, but hate what he did? This is exactly what Isaiah 1:14 and Amos 5:21 affirmed in connection with Israel's hypocritical worship as well. So, just as God loved Israel but could not stand what they did, so both Jacob and Esau were still loved as the rest of the context in Malachi 1:4–5 demonstrates: God had a future plan for Esau as well.

But just as the sinless Jesus was filled with indignation and anger in the days of the New Testament (Mark 3:5; 10:14; John 2:17; 11:33, 38), so in the Old Testament "hate" was the proper emotion for disavowing all evil and wrong that stood opposed to God and to all that was good. When a person truly and passionately stands for what was right, then their dislike and hatred of all that was wrong, evil, and wicked had to be opposed with all their being.

The antonyms "to love" (Hebrew, `*ahabah*) and "to hate" (Hebrew, *sin'ah*) are both used in Deuteronomy 21:15–17 to distinguish between the one loved and the one loved less. That same pair is found in the New Testament in Matthew 6:24 and Luke 16:13, where the Greek terms mean "to prefer" one over the other, or "to love" one more than the other are found. Therefore, in the case of Jacob and Esau, Jacob was called to a ministry of service, whereas Esau was not.

Nevertheless, Esau was not, therefore, an object of contempt, for he too would realize that God's promises in the present (Gen. 36:7), and his descendants in the future would also receive the deliverance of God (Obad. 19–21; Amos 9:12).

The Anger of God in the Prophets

It is a real shame that some have depicted the wrath of God as something that bordered on what is capricious, demonic, or as some sort of evidence for a type of a divine green-monster jealousy. The Jewish scholar Abraham Heschel explained how such embarrassment over the emotional aspects of biblical revelation caused the negative historical-critical school to adopt an evolutionary scheme for explaining the character of God. In their revised view of things, the God of the Old Testament exhibited demonic and primitive characteristics. To all of this Heschel commented:

> This view, which is neither true to fact nor in line with the fundamental biblical outlook, arises from a failure to understand the meaning of the God of pathos and particularly the meaning of anger as a mode of pathos. "Pathos," like its Latin equivalent *passio* from *pati* ("to suffer"), means a state of a condition in which something happens to man [sic], something of which it is a passive victim . . . emotions of pain or pleasure. We must not forget that the God of Israel is sublime rather than sentimental, nor should we associate the kind with the apathetic, the intense with the sinister, the dynamic with the demonic.[7]

"The Old Testament prophets," Heschel observed, "never thought of God's anger as something that cannot be accounted for, unpredictable, irrational."[8] For

---

7. Heschel, *The Prophets.* 2:27–28, 84.
8. Heschel, *The Prophets*, 2:62.

these prophets the anger of God was not blind, explosive, or without reference to the behavior of mortals. His anger was not to be treated in isolation from the surrounding circumstances and issues; instead, it was one of the ways in which God directly responded to men and women. It was conditioned mainly by God's will; it was aroused by the sin of humans. It was a secondary not a ruling passion in the character and nature of God. It would be more like what we sometimes regard all too lightly in ourselves and label it as "righteous indignation." Thus, to be impartial to people, God could not be indifferent to evil, for the divine being was pained and distressed when evil, sin, or injustice was done anywhere.

God's anger arises out of his care for humans. Moreover, in his use of his anger he never pitted his anger and mercy opposite one another; instead, anger and mercy were correlatives. As the prophet Habakkuk prayed, "In wrath remember mercy" (Hab. 3:2). It just could not be God, if his love should ever cease, as the Psalmist taught in Psalm 77:9: "Has God forgotten to be merciful? Has he in anger withheld his compassion?" Hardly! An example of this combination of anger and mercy could be found in Hosea 6:1–2: "Come, let us return to the LORD. He has torn us to pieces, but he will heal us; he has injured us but he will bind up our wounds. After two days he will revive us; on the third day he will restore us that we may live in his presence."

There is an evil that infects many humans, but it does not afflict God. It is the evil of indifference when we are in the presence of evil or wrongdoing. This evil often exists under a silent justification that is used to keep us from taking any kind of action against evil. The more we find rationalizations to avoid standing up to evil, the more likely it is that our toleration of evil is treated as the accepted thing to do. When God sees evil, however, there is an end to indifference to evil! God cannot treat wrong in an indifferent way, for to do so would mean that he would need to abdicate his rule and reign as God.

In order to understand the meaning of divine anger, it is necessary to reflect on the meaning of divine patience and divine forbearance. We have already mentioned that God is slow to anger, long-suffering, and patient, as witnessed in some ten Old Testament passages (Exod. 34:6; Num. 14:18; Neh. 9:17; Ps. 86:15; 103:8; 145:8; Jer. 15:15; Joel 2:13; Jonah 4:2; Nah. 1:3). But the divine patience must never be confused with some type of apathy or an attitude that can be swayed by the caprice of human beings, or even one that could be confused with overindulgence. Divine forgiveness must not be confused with unconditional forgiveness either for that would additionally lead to all sorts of evil. This is why the prophets repeatedly called for people to "amend [their] ways and [their] doings, obey the LORD . . . and repent of [their] evil" (Jer. 7:3; 26:13) as the grounds for receiving God's forgiveness.

To put it more directly, the anger of God is conditioned and subject to his will. Whenever the people whom the prophets addressed repented of the evil they had done, the mighty Lord of the universe changed in his threatened action towards these same individuals or nations. The declaration of the anger of God was not an announcement that judgment would immediately ensue; rather, it was a call to mortals to cancel the coming divine anger by obeying the injunctions given by the same prophets and to repent immediately.

Thus, there always was an aspect of contingency to God's anger. But this never represented a change in the nature and character of God; to the contrary, it affirmed just the reverse. Just as mortals can and do change when others who have occasioned our grief ask us to forgive them and to change our attitude towards them (thereby showing a continuity in our nature and character), just so God often demonstrates the same type of change in action, but not in his very nature. Nowhere is this pointed out more clearly than in Jeremiah 9:24—"I am the LORD, who exercises kindness, justice and righteousness on earth, for in these I delight, declares the LORD." Or again in Jeremiah 32:41, the prophet announced that the Lord commented: "I will delight in doing them good and will assuredly plant them in this land with all my heart and soul." This is the only time in Scripture where God assures us that what he has said is said "with all [God's] heart and soul."

Some have taken particular umbrage at those times when God's anger breaks out like a fire or a storm, as for example in Jeremiah 23:19–20: "See, the storm of the LORD will burst out in wrath, a whirlwind swirling down on the heads of the wicked. The anger of the LORD will not turn back until he fully accomplishes the purposes of his heart. In the days to come you will understand it clearly."

Some scholars have complained that on the bases of texts such as this one that God's anger is like a hidden force of nature, incalculable and arbitrary, as if it had no limits or mercy bound up with that anger. But such a conclusion is a distortion of the prophet's teaching, for God is never seen or represented as acting in an unaccountable way or in ways that cannot be explained. God's sense of outrage came over the people's mistreatment of the fatherless, the widow, and the poor. More fundamental to the attributes of God are his love and his mercy, but his anger is consistently represented as being transient and reactive to how the people are responding to his grace and his call to obey. Again, we need to be reminded that God's love or his kindness (*hesed*) go on forever (Jer. 33:11; Ps.

100:5; 106:1; 107:1; 118:1–4; 136:1–26), but we are never told that his anger likewise lasts forever! Instead, we are told that his anger lasts but for a moment (Ps. 30:5; Isa. 26:20; 57:7–8, 16–19). In fact, Israel had asked this very question: "Will you always be angry? Will your wrath continue forever?" (Jer. 3:5). To this straightforward inquiry God replied: "'Return, faithless Israel,' declares the Lord, 'I will frown on you no longer, for I am merciful,' declares the Lord, 'I will not be angry forever'" (Jer. 3:12). But Israel did not return to the Lord.

Heschel concludes his section on God's anger by declaring that "the secret of anger is God's care."[9] This is brought out clearly in Isaiah 12:1: "In that day you will say: 'I will praise you, O Lord. Although you were angry with me, your anger has turned away and you have comforted me.'"

The greatest comforting fact about God is that he really does care. Had it not been for God's caring, there would have been no story about Israel, no line of David from which the Messiah would come, and perhaps very little to speak of regarding the future. But God's caring made the difference. Therefore, Scripture teaches us to regard his anger and wrath not as irrational, emotional outbursts of the divine nature, but as part of his continual care. God's heart and being are not made out of stone, but his feelings are as real and tender as any we could ever imagine.

Moreover, the necessity of God's wrath and anger is actually distasteful to him; he would rather not be obligated to use it. This can be demonstrated from a number of passages, but especially from one we have already looked at—Hosea 11:9: "I will not carry out my fierce anger, nor will I turn and devastate Ephraim, For I am God and not man—the Holy One among you."

God must punish, but he cannot destroy his promises; indeed, he is in control and master of his anger and of his emotions. After all, He is God and not man!

Conclusion

There is no way anger can by any means be regarded as a distinguishing attribute of God, as if he had anger as one of his basic dispositions or as a quality that was inherent in his very nature that it existed separate from the rest of his attributes. Instead, his anger represents a mood, a state of mind and soul that is active towards sin and evil. It is never an uncontrolled spontaneous outburst, but it is always conditioned and under complete control by our Lord.

---

9.   Heschel, *The Prophets*, 2:72.

But God's anger is never to be seen as that which is the most lasting aspect of his responses to human beings for his mercy, grace, and kindness far outstrip anything we could attribute to his anger. The fact that wrongdoing excites his anger is a demonstration of his care for us for if he were indifferent, casual, and nonchalant about his wrath and his anger, then there would also be no assurance that when injustice, wrong, or evil were done to us that he would come to our rescue.

God's anger is preceded, as well as it is followed, by his love, grace, and mercy. It is for these reasons that we refuse to make a difference between the way God is represented in the Old Testament and the way he is represented in the New Testament. He is God, the Holy One, and not a man!

Discussion Questions

1. How do verses such as Isaiah 12:1 show that the secret to God's anger is that he still cares?

2. Which gives more delight to God: his anger or his kindness? What role do Jeremiah 9:24 and 32:41 play in answering this question?

3. Sometimes God's slowness to anger, his patience, and his long-suffering with sin and evil gets redefined as a form of divine apathy and caprice. How do you understand Exodus 34:6, Jonah 4:2, and Psalm 103:8 in light of this objection?

4. Has God ever once forgotten to be merciful (cf. Ps. 77:9; Hab. 3:2)?

5. How did Aristotle define anger versus the way this concept is used of God's anger?

6. Is God passible or impassible in his emotions?

2

The God of Peace or the God of Ethnic Cleansing?

Question: *Is God the God who ordered the geno-cide of the Canaanites or is he the God of peace?*

Quite a few readers of the Bible, especially some of the younger postmodern surveyors of the Scripture, declare that the Old Testament is not for them since it is a book full of wars, violence, and divinely authorized genocide. How can such a state of affairs exist when the God of the New Testament is a God of peace and love? God cannot be both loving and genocidal at the same time, can he? The fact that the Old Testament records such an excessive amount of wars and violence seems to be contrary to the love principle taught in that same Bible, especially as God is presented in the New Testament. Is God's manner and attitude in the Old Testament, then, just the opposite of his depiction as a God of love, mercy, and grace in the New Testament?

There is no doubt that almost every generation has been seriously affected by wide-scale violence. Young adults today remember vividly the horrific collapse of the World Trade Center towers on September 11, 2001 and the deaths of almost three thousand Americans and other nationalities from some ninety nations around the world. Many older Americans who lived through the attack on Pearl Harbor in 1941 felt a sense deja vu on 9/11.

For most Americans, the images of 9/11—the two hijacked airliners filled with innocent passengers plowing into the World Trade Center towers; causing the horrible inferno from which some occupants of the towers leaped to their deaths to escape immolation; the unimaginable collapse of the towers, taking hundreds of lives, including fire, police, and medical responders; the charred remains of two airliners whose passengers died in another attack on the Pentagon and a fourth crash near Shanksville, Pennsylvania—these scenes of senseless and wanton brutality will not be quickly erased from their minds and hearts. These were acts of war at its worst. How could this have happened? Where was God when it all transpired? Did God approve of such violence?

Some who read descriptions of violence in the Old Testament experience much the same feelings as those felt during 9/11. The violence in the conquest of Canaan, for example, seems to run counter to the most common descriptions of God in the Bible. Such descriptions of his character stress his compassion, his grace, and his love. God's love is presented as being without any boundaries except those of his own character. How can we explain, then, such seeming violent brutality in the Old Testament, as well as come to grips with the violent horrors that are in our world today?

While the Bible does lay heavy emphasis on God's love and mercy, it is not afraid to show us the other side of his character as well: His wrath and his warnings about judgment to those who walk contrary to his word. These are just as much a part of the divine person as is his mercy and his love! So the two aspects of his character must not be confused, but neither should they be separated, as we will see in what follows.

Even though the issue of whether war is, in principle, "right" or "wrong" is never by itself directly addressed in the Bible, it is not correct to assume that all wars in the older text of the Bible were events that the Lord approved of or that he wanted to be identified with them as their sponsor. It is true that the verb "to make war" (Hebrew, *nilham*) occurs some 164 times (in the Hebrew Niphal stem [usually a passive form of the verb in Hebrew]), and the noun form, "war" (Hebrew, *milhamah*), appears about 320 times in the Old Testament. Such a high frequency of use makes war a prominent part of the biblical narrative. The greater number of these wars and Israel's battles occurred in the wilderness following the exodus from Egypt and the subsequent conquest of Canaan or in Israel's conflicts with surrounding nations in the Near East, such as the Amalekites, the Philistines, the Syrians, the Assyrians, the Babylonians, and the Medo-Persians.

In light of these basic statistics, how is the Lord himself represented in these contests? Does he play a role in some or even in all of them, and, if so, what is that role?

Yahweh As Warrior[1]

As early in the biblical text as Exodus 15:1–18, Yahweh (God) is portrayed as a warrior, one who leads his people into battle and fights for them. God's deliverance of Israel from Egypt is the first time that he demonstrated this aspect of his character. Thereafter, Yahweh's role as "warrior" became the model and paradigm for those battles that would follow, in which Israel put her trust in the Lord to lead them when war was approved by God. But Yahweh's appearance in such wars did not mean that he gave Israel, or even later generations, an open invitation to enter into any or all wars without regard to any conditions whatsoever. Instead, wars could only be entered into at Yahweh's explicit direction and instruction and if they met Yahweh's criteria.

What about the war upon the Canaanites then? Did God authorize Israel's attack on the land of Canaan, and was every battle in the conquest of the land approved by God? The answer, of course, is that not every battle Israel ever fought or any war that the other nations wanted to engage in was approved by God. There had to be a reason for Yahweh to direct Israel to go to war. In the case of the Canaanites, we know that the Lord has waited for four hundred years until the sins of the Canaanites finally mounted up so that the Canaanites filled the cup of judgment. God had been watching all those years to see if the Canaanites would repent and turn from their evil (Gen. 15:13–16).

How Wicked Were the Canaanites?

Yahweh certainly was not precipitous or in any rush to inflict judgment on anyone. In the case of the Canaanites, as we just noted, God waited four hundred years until "the sin of the Amorite[s]—a Canaanite people group—had "reached its limit" (Gen. 15:13, 16). Therefore, even back into the days of Abraham, the Canaanites had not yet provided enough evidence for the judgment of God or for the land to "vomit them out" (Lev. 18:25). Yet over against the Canaanites, the cities of Sodom and Gomorrah proved that they were more than ready for God's judgment at an even earlier date (c. 1800–1900 bc), since not even ten righteous people could be found in those cities to delay their just punishment of God (Gen. 18–19).

Going back to an even earlier period, it was clear that not even the preaching of Noah for 120 years produced one bit of change in those who ultimately

---

1. See Patrick D. Miller, Jr., "God the Warrior," *Interpretation,* 19 (1965): 39–46.

perished in the flood (Gen. 6:3; Noah is called "a preacher of righteousness" in 2 Peter 2:5). In that case as well, God waited to see if anyone would repent as a result of Noah's preaching. Only seven of Noah's family members heeded and responded to Noah's preaching. That was a very small response for what appeared to be 120 years of Noah's exhortations (1 Peter 3:18–21)!

So what was so horrible about the Canaanites that also caused their condemnation? In the Ugaritic literature, found in Ras Shamra, Syria (from which we get our earliest alphabetic script from c. 1400–1200 BC), we are given a picture of what was going on in that culture of that time. Similar to the gods they worshiped, they too were guilty of incest and all types of social and sexual wickedness. For example, they, in imitation of their gods, were involved in bestiality, homosexual acts, temple sex, and even child sacrifice. Instead of reflecting the image of the true God, the Canaanites reflected the image of the gods and goddesses they worshiped, thinking that by acting as the gods and goddesses acted, there would be some sort of magical help that would produce fertility, not only in humans but in their animals and crops as well.

Thus, the goddess Anath, who was the patroness of both sex and war, cut a ruthless figure of violence and immorality for the people to imitate. In one of Anath's massacre scenes, the following description portrays her brutality (as translated by William Foxwell Albright):

> The blood was so deep that she waded in it up to her knees—nay, up to her neck. Under her feet were human heads, above her human hands flew like locusts. In her sensuous delight she decorated herself with suspended heads while she attached hands to her girdle. Her joy at the butchery is described in even more sadistic language. "Her liver swelled with laughter, her heart was full of joy, the liver of Anath [was full of] exultation (?)." Afterwards Anath "was satisfied" and washed her hands in human gore before proceeding to other occupations. [2]

Seen in this light, even granting in part for the use of hyperbolic language, Canaanite religion was not simply a personal affair; it was a worldview that affected all society in the land where Israel was called to dwell. In no way did

---

2. William Foxwell Albright, *Archaeology and the Religion of Israel* (Baltimore: Johns Hopkins Press, 1968), 77.

Yahweh want his people to be corrupted by such lifestyles and religion; Israel must be separate and live holy lives.

Even so, some will still object, "Is it not true that other nations present just as good a cause or reason for God to judge them as well?" What made the attack on Canaan and the eradication of the whole nation justifiable? Were they so much more evil than any other nation in the world that they had to be obliterated? In other words, what was it in their case that showed they had reached the point of no return, that the cup of their iniquity had at last been filled to overflowing?

God was not unfairly picking on the Canaanites, nor was he demonstrating that he was intolerant for he did command all peoples worldwide that they should have "no other gods before [him]." This was not an act that showed a lack of tolerance, for there was no other God in addition to Yahweh; this was a plain fact. Moreover, Yahweh judged all nations, not because they failed to worship him; rather, they were judged, as Amos 1–2 reminded us, for their outrageous immoral acts that violated the very character and norms established by God. God was not only offended by the nations surrounding Israel and Judah and acted in judgment on them, he acted the same way toward Israel and Judah for the same reasons. In fact, Deuteronomy 1:10 and 20 indicate that God had disposed of several other nations before the Canaanites from those very same territories for the very same reasons. And that is how our Lord continues to act toward nations today, for this story gets repeated over and over again in the rest of Israel's history.

In addition to this, it was always Yahweh who informed Moses, Samuel, and Joshua when the time was right to move out for battle if the situation legitimately called for conquest. (Num. 14:41–45; Josh. 7; 1 Sam. 4). In fact, the situation of the Canaanites was unique to Israel and Judah. This should not be taken as a universal call that was to be operative for all times, all cultures and all peoples, or for whenever nations wished to go to war with other nations. The question as to whether the war was right or wrong still had to be answered, and that answer had to pass muster with a holy and righteous God.

One might object that the Canaanites should not to be blamed for what they were practicing in their pagan idolatry for how could they have acted any differently since they were perhaps untaught? Was not what they practiced the best "theology" they knew, some will say. So why were they held to what seemed to be a higher standard without being given the chance to hear the good news of the gospel that had been given to Abraham (Gen. 12:3; Gal. 3:8)?

The apostle Paul would not have accepted that argument or any variation of it. He asked of all pagans, in Romans 1:19–20, "Have they not all heard?" What could be known about God was evidently written within them, for they too were made in God's image. In fact, even God's invisible attributes, including his "eternal power and divine nature [were visible to them], . . . so that they [were] without excuse." The process for determining right and wrong did not begin with the Mosaic Law code, but it began with their own in-built consciences. There also was the teaching about the Messiah; this was the good news for all the people on earth!

As if to give an example of this truth, the Bible records the story of Rahab, the prostitute in the city of Jericho, who overcame her thorough-going pagan, Canaanite upbringing and claimed her faith in the God of Israel, based on what she had heard of Israel's deliverance through the Red Sea and Israel's victories over Pharaoh, King Sihon, and King Og on the other side of the Jordan River (Josh. 2). Rahab purposely broke with the established traditions and beliefs of her pagan upbringing to order to place her faith in the Lord, and as a result she was placed in the list of the "heroes of faith" in Hebrews 11. It was possible, therefore, for a pagan to believe in Messiah and to follow what was right. Rahab is a witness to that fact.

Some objectors, however, will continue to protest: wasn't this Canaanite invasion simply another instance of "ethnic cleansing" and "genocide?" Richard Dawkins, the contemporary neo-atheist, argues for this conclusion, claiming that these acts of war carried out by Israel were done with a "xenophobic relish." But such hyped language adds liabilities to the discussion that were not in the biblical text in the first place. There is no evidence that Israel's conquest was stirred up by racial hatred, which is what the charge of "ethnic cleansing" and "xenophobia" imply. Nor is there evidence that Israel "relished" waging war with Canaan! From the very beginning of the biblical story, the promise and blessing given to Abraham and his descendants included the goal that "all the families of the earth" would be blessed by means of the promised blessing given to Abraham though his "Seed" (Gen. 12:3). However, for those who would curse Israel (presumably not just because they were Israelites, but because they were representatives of God's promise-plan on earth), would themselves be cursed, for God took those curses as curses that were leveled against him personally as well as against Israel! In other words, to attack Israel was tantamount to attacking God.

God clearly disapproved of all forms of racism or ethnocentrism. In fact, the Old Testament has one foreigner after another being made part of the central story in the promise-plan of God. For example, Melchizedek is a priest-king in the Canaanite city of Salem (identified with Jerusalem) in Genesis 14, yet Abraham paid tithes to him and received God's word from his lips and actions. Again, as Israel left Egypt, a "mixed multitude" (Exod. 12:38) was part of Israel's entourage, which meant that a good number of Egyptians put their faith in Israel's God and left Egypt with Israel. Later, after his first wife died, Moses married a dark-skinned Cushite woman (Num. 12:1), to the discomfort of some Israelites but not to God's displeasure. We could also include Ruth, the Moabite, who became part of the Messianic line or the previously mentioned Canaanite prostitute, Rahab, who was also part of that famous ancestry of Jesus' heritage.

Add to these examples the divine command that Israel was to show particular care and concern for aliens and sojourners who would come into the land (Lev. 19:34; Deut. 10:18–19), because Israel had at one point been in the same position in Egypt as Pharaoh's slaves in a foreign country. The law of God specifically directed that "There shall be one standard for you; it shall be the same for the stranger as well as the native, for I am Yahweh your God." The alien was included in the covenant of God for they too were to participate in the Passover (Num. 9:14). A dual standard or a claim of xenophobia of any sort was totally ruled out of order by the clear teaching of Scripture. Immigrants were to be accepted, not treated with disdain.

Even though the language of the Israelite conquest sounds very much like a total eradication of the Canaanite population including all men, women and children, it is important to allow for the presence of traditional Near Eastern hyperbole in their "war-talk," which frequently occurs in other battle descriptions from neighboring countries that surrounded Israel. A term in the Bible, which catches this special nuance, focuses on "driving out" the Canaanites (Hebrew, *garash,* "to drive out"). For example, before Israel invaded the land, already in Exodus 23:29, 31, God had warned: "But I will not drive them [Canaanites] out in a single year." And, "I will hand over to you the people who live in the land and you will drive them out before you." The same theology is found in Joshua 24:12: "I sent the hornet ahead of you, which drove them [Canaanites] out before you." Again in Joshua 24:18: "And the LORD drove out before us all the nations, including the Amorites, who lived in the land." Therefore, before a quick judgment is made about a so-called "ethnic cleansing" of all Canaanites by the edge of the sword, it must be realized that other types of forces from Yahweh were also at work, if not even more effective than what had been realized in the use of warfare by Israel.

The New Testament as well can hardly be classified as a "pacifist" book that contrasts with the Old Testament. Compare its texts about the future use of war in the end times (Mark 13:7; Rev. 6:3–8; 19:11–21) with Old Testament pronouncements. The language found in the New Testament is also taken from the sphere of war and conjures up scenes very similar to those in the Old Testament. Thus, all attempts to make a distinction between the two testaments on the matter of war seem to be doomed to failure from the start.

Some might maintain that the Bible merely records—but does not legitimize—the actions of humans in the wars recorded in the Bible. Such facile explanations, however, will hardly settle all the issues that must be dealt with on the topic of war in the Bible, in ancient history, or in modern times. That is why it is also impossible to claim, as some want to do, that the rules of warfare noted in Scripture are the result of the opinions of various redactors of the Bible, who are mirroring their own views and the foreign influences of the day. Of the approximately five dozen wars or battles described in the Bible (everything from Abraham's rescue of Lot in Genesis 14 to the Babylonian destruction of Jerusalem), a dozen or so are directly identified as "wars of Yahweh." How are we to understand these? God has often revealed himself in his word on the subject of war just as clearly as he has continued to reveal himself on other matters as well. So let's look at the text of Scripture to see what it actually teaches on this subject of war.

Israel's "Manual of War"

Even before Israel began her conquest of Canaan, God had instructed Moses in Deuteronomy 20:1–20 on the rules of warfare. This is one of the key texts on the subject of war in the Old Testament. The chief difference between Israel and her neighbors was that Israel was never allowed to expand her territories by conquering the land occupied by her surrounding nations. Any and all approved movements of the military that took Israel into the battle were solely to be at the direction of the Lord, not the idea of a military general or king in Israel or Judah. In fact, Israel had no need to prove her greatness by her military might or prowess for her greatness was to be found first and last in the fact that Yahweh was her God. Therefore, Israel had nothing else to prove by conquering new territories in order to enhance the nation's reputation and status. Neither were her wars to be known as a "holy wars" or something similar to the Medieval ideas of a Christian "Crusade" or a Muslim "Jihad." Israel's wars were to be known as "Yahweh Wars" (Deut. 20:1–4). Israel had nothing to prove by conquering others; she was to be directed by the Lord in all such endeavors. Israel did not even own the land in which she lived for the land of Israel itself also belonged to the Lord. Israel only possessed the land on sort of a long-term "lease" arrangement, but its real owner was Yahweh.

Deuteronomy 20 contains instructions on how the nation was to conduct war and is best divided into two sections: verses 1–15, which contains rules for ordinary war, and verses 16–20, which sets forth rules for "Yahweh Wars."

Surprisingly, Deuteronomy 20 doesn't come off as a shrill militaristic creed—it is actually more anti-militaristic in its tone and its instructions. For example, it calls for a considerable reduction in the size of the army and the repeated release of those who were probably the most fit and youngest of the soldiers. Several types of exemptions from military duty were given:

1. for men who had just built a house (v. 5)
2. for men who had planted a vineyard but not received as yet any fruit from it (v. 6)
3. for men who were just engaged to be married (v. 7)
4. for men who were in their first year of marriage (v. 7)
5. those men who were just plain "spooked" about going into battle (v. 8)

Rather than allowing these latter men to spread discouragement, defeat, and discontent among the troops, they were all to be released immediately from military duty and sent back home. That certainly seems counterintuitive if one was trying to foster military strength in numbers.

Cities or countries that Israel met in battle *outside* Canaan were to be offered terms of peace first, before any battle began (vs. 10, 15) while those *inside* the land of Canaan were to be "driven out" of the land and defeated due to their accumulated wickedness over the centuries, which had by Joshua's time mounted up to high heaven (Deut. 7:1–6; 25–26). God had patiently waited for some four hundred years until the "cup [of Canaan's] iniquity" was full. God had waited to see if the "cup of [the nation's] iniquity" would slacken or would be filled up (Gen. 15:13, 16).

An ecological sensitivity had to be exercised by Israel's troops as well during the exercise of the war so that fruit trees were not chopped down or destroyed, or used to build siege ramps, or employed for acts of destruction (Deut. 20:19–20). Also, captive women were to be shown mercy. If such a woman were to marry an Israelite, she could never be sold or treated as a slave.

The rules in this chapter are reminiscent of some of the modern rules of war in the Geneva Convention. The rules for warfare in Deuteronomy differ significantly from what passed as standard practice of the day. While Israel was not allowed to engage in imperialistic acts of land-grabbing warfare, wars were still one of the realities of that day. Deuteronomy 20:1 made it clear that Israel's power was not to reside in her horses, chariots, or mammoth armies. Even though the Israelites were "the fewest of all peoples" (Deut. 7:7), their strength was to rest in the Lord, and not in the strength or amount of their military personnel, military hardware, or military achievements as was common in their day.

The Justification of "Yahweh Wars" in the Old Testament

How are we to justify, then, what appears to be instances of "ethnic cleansing" or "genocide" carried out against the six to ten nations who occupied the land of Canaan prior to Israel's invasion of the land? And how are we to understand this in light of Jesus' teaching that Israel, and we, are to love our enemies as taught especially in the New Testament (but also in the Old Testament as well)? Two different paths seem to be set up by these quotes in many contemporary minds as a clear contradiction between the two testaments, but is this distinction fair to the text? In fact, this contradiction can be summed up in Jesus' Sermon on the Mount. There he reported what was currently being said by the common people—"hate your enemy"—but Jesus countered with: "Love your neighbor . . . love your enemies and pray for those who persecute you" (Matt. 5:43–44).

First of all, as hinted at above, God was the chief and only protagonist in each of the "Yahweh Wars" that Israel and Judah carried out. It was God who conceived of the war, who commanded it, and who brought it to its conclusion. Without the guiding and planning hand of God in these contests, Israel would have been left defeated and beaten time and time again. Just as God would often use the hands of other nations to punish Israel when they continued to stray from him (see Isa. 10:5, 15), so God also would use the hands of Israel to punish Gentile nations that violated what Yahweh and his character stood for.

It was also necessary for the troops of Israel to be spiritually prepared and sanctified. To begin with, any battle had to start with consultation and direction from God. Failure to do so would be a recipe for disaster for Israel right from the start, as Joshua soon learned in his meeting with the Gibeonites in Joshua 9:14 —"The Israelites sampled [the Gibeonites] provisions but they did not inquire of the LORD."

In that case, Joshua's fault, along with that of the leaders of Israel, was that "they examined the empirical evidence but they did not consult the LORD" (Josh. 9:14). They trusted their own rational senses and critical abilities rather than going to the Lord in prayer to ask for his guidance. As a result, they were hoodwinked by the fabricated story that the Gibeonites concocted in order to protect them from Israel.

Israel was never allowed to just start a battle any time they wanted to for as long as God was excluded from their plans, they were to refrain from any humanly motivated or authorized excuse for going into battle. That divine direction usually came in one of two ways: 1) The Lord would either give a divine command; or 2) an inquiry was to be made of God by means of the use of an oracle from God. For example, the first kind of direction can be seen as Joshua prepared to enter Canaan. There he was met by the enigmatic figure, who appeared in front of him with a drawn sword (Josh. 5:13–15). Joshua asked, "Are you for us or against us?" The man with the drawn sword answered: He had come as "Commander of the Lord's Army." In response Joshua reverently removed the sandals from his feet, just as Moses had done at the burning bush in the desert (Exod. 3). It was clear that this figure was none other than a pre-incarnate form of the Lord himself, who thereby commissioned Joshua and set forth a strategy for the forthcoming battle for Canaan.

At other times, as preparation for battle or as an inquiry into how the battle should proceed, the king would ask the priest to bring the ephod and make inquiry of God for a divine oracle as to whether the army should attack or should retreat, much as David did in the famous episode at Keilah in Samuel 23. David would not dare to make a move militarily without investigating and learning what was the mind of God prior to initiating any military action.

On the other hand, the episode at the town of Ai illustrates the consequences of a failure to consult God. After Israel's triumph over the mighty city of Jericho, it hardly seemed worthwhile to consult or to bother God, over such a small rural town with such a slight population as the town of Ai. But that turned into a tragic miscalculation for an act of sin in the camp, during the previous campaign, now caused the defeat of Israel. An Israelite soldier named Achan had stolen from the loot in the town of Jericho that had been "totally dedicated" to God, which he had hidden in his tent. Since the whole town of Jericho had been "totally dedicated" (Hebrew, *herem*)[3] to the Lord, noth-

---

3.   Philip D. Stern, *The Biblical Herem: A Window on Israel's Religious Experience*. (Atlanta: Scholars Press, 1991).

ing was to be taken and used personally. It belonged in a very particular and specific way to the Lord. But Achan disobeyed the order and thus he brought tragedy on the whole camp.

In most military ventures, everything depends on the military prepared-ness of the troops, but for Israel spiritual preparation took priority over physical training or equipping the army with proper hardware or exercise. For instance, before the battle of Jericho could be fought, Israel had to observe the Passover and all the males, who had failed to be circumcised during the forty-year wilder-ness journey, were now to comply with this ordinance of circumcision. Surpris-ingly, this had to be accomplished even though they were so close to engaging the enemy at Jericho, and the men would be temporarily unable to bear arms for several days until they had healed. But first things had to come first!

Often it was necessary to offer sacrifices before a battle began, as in 1 Sam-uel 13 where Saul waited for the tardy Samuel to arrive and offer the sacrifice. Overly anxious and exhausted by the stress of waiting, Saul arrogantly took up the priestly duties and autocratically offered the sacrifices to the Lord, only to be roundly scolded by Samuel when he finally appeared. It is important to note, however, that for Israel it was to be a fearsome thing to enter into battle without sacrificing to God and to receive his authorization for entering into the battle and his promise of his deliverance.

Since the Lord himself was directing the army, it was necessary that the men all be ritually clean and holy as set apart to God. When David asked for the bread of presence from the Tabernacle (ordinarily used exclusively by the priests) to feed the rogue army that accompanied him, the priest Ahimelech wanted to know if the men were holy and had kept themselves from women (1 Sam. 21:5); otherwise the men would have been unable to share in eating the bread. In the same way, the soldier Uriah, even though he was a Hittite mercenary in David's army refused to be lured by King David into going home to sleep with his wife (which David intended as a cover for his adultery with Bathsheba), despite David's continual insistence that he take advantage of the opportunity. Even though Uriah was unaware of what had happened between David and his wife, if had he gone home and slept with his wife, he would also have temporarily disqualified himself from the battle line. Leviticus 15:1–18 forbade a man from approaching God after an emission of semen, even though that emission came in the normal and approved action of marital intercourse. Uriah would have been unclean for twenty-four hours and therefore could not approach God or his work on the battlefield, despite the impending battle. In such a condition, he would have disqualified himself from going immediately back to the battlefield, for he would have been spiritually unfit for such duties.

The Reason for the Divine Genocide of the Canaanites

Given the fact that God is omnipotent and sovereign, he can accomplish his purposes in any or all ways that he pleases and which are also in keeping with his character. Therefore, because God is holy, long periods of national opposition to his holiness by the enemy (or by Israel) must finally be dealt with. So it was that Abraham was promised that his descendants would return back to the land after their future exile from that land because of their unrepentant sin. They would return to the very land where Abraham had previously received God's covenant in Genesis 15 after four generations of being away from the land while slaves in Egypt (Gen. 15:16). The seven to ten nations that occupied the land at that time included the Kenites, Kenizzites, Kadmonites, Hittites, Perizzites, Rephaites, Amorites, Canaanites, Girgashites, and Jebusites. They would all be removed by military force from that land (Gen. 15:19–21), when the sin of those ten nations had "reached its full measure" (Gen. 15:16). Elsewhere the Canaanite nations are variously numbered and listed as being eleven in number (Gen. 10:15–18), ten (Exod. 15:19–21), seven (as in this passage), six (Exod. 3:8; 33:2), and even just three (Exod. 23:28). But the list usually referred to all the same groups, even if the lists were not always exhaustive or comprehensive.

The word that was used to indicate that the judgment of these nations had arrived was the fact that they were now under the "ban" (*herem*), a Hebrew word used about eighty times in the Old Testament. This word has not been found so far in Ugaritic, a Canaanite language that shares about sixty percent of the same vocabulary with Hebrew, but it appears in all the other Semitic languages. Thus, the famous Moabite Stone[4] used the word *herem* on lines 14–17 to indicate that the King of Moab "devoted" (*harem*) to destruction seven thousand of his citizens of the city of Nebo to his god Chemosh as an offering to achieve victory in battle.

---

4   The Mesha Stele (the "Moabite Stone") is an inscribed stone from the ninth century BC, commissioned by king of Moab, a kingdom located east of the Dead Sea. It contains a parallel account of events recorded in 2 Kings 3:4–8 from the Moabite viewpoint. Discovered in 1868, it is the longest Iron Age inscription discovered from the area to date and provides valuable insights into the Moabite language.

In Arabic, the word was used originally of the "enclosure" or courtyard that set aside for the king's wives, his "harem." In the Akkadian language it was also used to mean a "prostitute" in the sense of that a woman was totally dedicated or set apart in the service of a god. But in all its usages, it indicated a "separation," something that was "set aside for one's exclusive use" (often in a total sense) or, in these national contexts, it meant "set aside for total destruction."

This setting aside of *herem* was always an *involuntary* dedication or separation. In that sense, then, it is the opposite of one who *voluntarily* dedicates one's whole self or sets one's total self aside, as in Romans 12:12, as a whole sacrifice to God. Those who were under the "ban," were marked for an *involuntary* dedication. It was a forced dedication and thus resembled a "curse" that was laid on one's enemies at the direction of God. Those who harbored idolaters, the disobedient, law-breakers, or those who hated God would be treated similar to those cities or nations that were also "dedicated to destruction"—cities such as Jericho (Josh. 6:21); Ai (Josh. 8:26); Makkedah (Josh. 10:28); and Hazor (Josh. 11:11). The rationale for this type of divine "dedication to destruction" is given in Deuteronomy 7:1–6, which reads:

> When the LORD your God brings you into the land you are entering to possess and drives out before you many nations—the Hittites, Girgashites, Amorites, Canaanites, Perizzites, Hivites, and Jebusites, seven nations larger and stronger than you—and when the LORD your God has delivered them over to you and you have defeated them, then you must destroy them totally [*herem*]. Make no treaty with them, and show them no mercy. Do not intermarry with them. Do not give your daughters to their sons or take their daughters for your sons, for they will turn your sons away from following me to serve other gods, and the LORD's anger will burn against you and will quickly destroy you. This is what you are to do to them: Break down their altars, smash their sacred stones, cut down their Asherah poles and burn their idols in the fire. For you are a people holy to the LORD your God. The LORD your God has chosen you out of all the peoples on the face of the earth to be his people, his treasured possession.

Israel was to live in the land, but not let the land begin to live in them. Israel was not to tolerate idolatrous practices or compromise with the inhabitants of the land. Her sole allegiance was to be to the Lord. Israel was to be God's special jewel, his moveable treasure. All tarnishes in that single ornament were to be removed for any type of eclectic acting and thinking amounted to treason to the God they called "Lord."

Another set of concepts associated with "Yahweh Wars" is "vengeance and revenge." It was George E. Mendenhall who gave us the definitive study on this word "vengeance" (*naqam*) in the Old Testament.[5] Of the seventy-eight instances where this verb occurs in the Old Testament, fifty-one of them involve Yahweh as the actor; indeed, the classical statement of this concept is in Deuteronomy 32:35, 41—"It is mine to avenge. . . . I will take vengeance on my adversaries."

There are two ways in which God takes "vengeance" on persons, cities, or nations:

1.   God is the people's champion against their enemies (Ps. 94).
2.   God punishes covenant-breakers (Lev. 26:24–25).

In both of these usages, it is the use of God's power that is the common feature, whether that power is internal or external. It does not, however, carry the idea of a repayment in kind of any unrighteousness or injustice. On the contrary, God holds back his vengeance for a long time in that he is slow to anger (Nah. 1:2–3). But even though he restrains his anger, yet his holiness must finally express itself as a disapproval of the persons or nations that fail to live up to or act in his righteousness.

The problem with the word "vengeance" is the common way that we use the word today. In contemporary usage vengeance means "to get even" with those who have treated us wrongfully. But God is never jealous with green envy toward others about anything nor does he need to try to get even with others. Since he is God, there is no need to think about being on an even plane with anything or anyone else. What motivates him to act in these cases is his "zeal" for his name, his holiness and his purity, not a sense of trying to "get even," or to "pay back" someone for provoking him or doing him in (see chapter 1 on God's wrath for more detail on this point).

At the end of the conquest of Canaan, Joshua could summarize the whole sweep of his victories in Canaan in Joshua 23 by saying that the conquest origi-

---

5.   George E. Mendenhall, "The Vengeance of Yahweh," in *The Tenth Generation* (Baltimore: Johns Hopkins University Press, 1973), 69–104.

nated and was carried out by Yahweh himself. The Lord had fought for the Israelites and had given the land to them.

> You yourselves have seen everything the Lord your God has done to all these nations for your sake; it was the Lord your God who fought for you. Remember how I have allotted as an inheritance for your tribes all the land of the nations that remain—nations I conquered—between the Jordan and the Great Sea in the west. The Lord your God himself will drive them out of your way. He will push them out before you, and you will take possession of their land, as the Lord your God promised you (vs. 3–5).

> The Lord has driven out before you great and powerful nations; to this day no one has been able to withstand you. One of you routs a thousand, because the Lord your God fights for you, just as he promised (vs. 9–10).

Later the Old Testament prophets would affirm that the conquest of Canaan was the powerful work of God and not the work of human hands (e.g., Amos 2:9; Hos. 2:14–15). Even in the New Testament, Stephen and Paul declared the conquest was an act of God's sovereignty (Acts 7:45; 13:19).

Some have tried to avoid the issue of violence in the Old Testament by saying that the Israelites *thought* that God had commanded them to clear the land of all Canaanites, but they were wrong in attributing it to Yahweh. This view is set forth with fervor by C. S. Cowles, but he bases his case on examples that cannot be used of the conquest.[6] For example, he illustrates it by pointing to the fact that Moses killed an Egyptian, which he thought was correct (which it wasn't), but he ended up fleeing for his life. But Moses never was instructed by God to murder that Egyptian. Or, Cowles uses the example of the prophet Nathan telling David to build the temple for God, but then he had to come back and say that God never said he was to build the temple in the first place; however, Nathan was expressing his own desire, so to speak, and he spoke "off the cuff" on his own initiative and not as the oracle of God. Nathan did not say, "Thus says the Lord" to David. Later that night God came to him, and so he was

---

6. C. S. Cowles, "The Case for Radical Discontinuity," in *Show Them No Mercy: Four Views on God and Canaanite Genocide,* ed. Stanley N. Gundry (Grand Rapids: Zondervan, 2003), 13–44.

able to say the next day, "Thus says the Lord." But in the case of the conquest, too many times the text directly informs us that it all was accomplished by the will and plan of God with his own personal involvement.

"Yahweh War" in the *Eschaton* of the New Testament

While Jesus makes no direct mention of anything like "Yahweh Wars," the Apocalypse, or New Testament book of Revelation, has a number of scenes that are not all that different from the depth of destruction and violence described in the wars waged in the Old Testament. For instance, witness the riders who go forth on the four horses in Revelation 6:1–8 to wreak a terrific amount of havoc on planet earth—yet they are all divinely appointed.

In the battle scene of Revelation 12:7–17, an enormous red dragon, who is identified as the Devil, tries to destroy a child born to a woman, but the child is taken up into heaven in an escape. This all leads to the armies of heaven going to war with Satan. This is war on a cosmic scale between God and Satan.

In another famous battle scene known as the battle of Armageddon in Revelation 16:12–16 and 19:11–21, a battle takes place in Israel on the "great day of the Lord." Once again the Lord leads the armies of heaven, only this time he is on a white horse as he crushes the assembled armies from all the nations on earth.

One more great war that might be mentioned here takes place in Revelation 20:7–10 where Satan is released from his confinement, being bound in chains for almost a millennium, only to face a devastating blow from the armies of God and to be finally consigned to an everlasting hell.

So there is a case to be made that in the New Testament we see the same type of battles with the Lord himself as the protagonist as we see in the Old Testament. But there is no justification for saying that Christ's church has any authority for reintroducing the "Yahweh Wars" of the Old Testament during this current era of time.

However, at the same time, such a conclusion is not thereby a support for some form of Christian pacifism in this present era either. War is not systematically or roundly condemned in and of itself, for there are situations in which the cry for justice necessitates the rebuke of dictatorships and abusive governments. These issues must be addressed with force and even by war itself when all other means have been tried and have failed. That is why God has established human government (Rom. 13:1–7), and that is why they come equipped bearing swords. Yet they too must depend on the direction of God in the cause of goodness and justice.

The Christian and Jihad

Some have incorrectly referred to "Yahweh Wars" in the Old Testament by the title of "holy wars" as mentioned above, but it must be stated that they are never so designated in either testament.[7] However, the term "holy war" has come back into vogue with the use of the Arabic word *jihad* by Islamic terrorists. Some Arabic and Islamic scholars have argued that this *jihad* in the Qur'an means "an inner spiritual struggle," not war. Most scholars point out that in some contexts in the Qur'an, it clearly does mean taking an aggressive military action for the defense or the propagation of the Muslim faith.

Some passages in the Qur'an advocate a pacifist position in the face of controversy, such as Sura (chapter) 15:94–95. But Sura 9:5 clearly calls for a militant *jihad* against unbelievers: "When the forbidden months are past, fight and slay the idolaters wherever you find them, and seize them, beleaguer them, and lie in wait for them in every stratagem [of war]; but if they repent and establish regular prayers and pay alms tax, then open the way for them, for God is oft-forgiving, most merciful."[8] Accordingly, the use of violent force to make all the world subservient to Islam is clearly approved in this Sura.

Conclusion

There is no justification for what is called "holy war" or *jihad* in the Bible. Instead, believers must sharply distinguish between "Yahweh Wars" and so-called Islamic "holy wars." They represent two different genres of war.

Moreover, the problem with "Yahweh Wars" in the Old Testament is mainly a problem with God. It is Yahweh himself who starts and carries out such wars. But he is the same God who reveals himself as holy, righteous, just and merciful.

---

7. Ben C. Ollenburger, "Introduction," in Gerhard von Rad, *Holy War in Ancient Israel*, ed. and trans. Marva J. Dawn (Grand Rapids: Eerdmans, 1991); G. H. Jones, "The Concept of Holy War," in *The World of Ancient Israel*, ed. R. E. Clements (Cambridge: Cambridge Univ. Press, 1989), 313–14.
8. Reuven Firestone, "Conceptions of Holy War in Biblical and Qur'anic Tradition," *Journal of Religious Ethics* 24 (1996): 108–15.

Without always resolving just how his anger over sin and deliberate unrighteousness is balanced with his attributes of grace, love, mercy and kindness, the record nevertheless supports both aspects of his character.

What God does in the exercise of both his justice and his mercy is good. We correctly affirm that "God loves the sinner but he hates his sin." C. S. Lewis at first commented negatively on such an aphorism:

> I remember Christian teachers telling me long ago that I must hate a bad man's actions but not hate the bad man: or, as they would say, hate the sin but not the sinner. . . . I used to think this a silly, straw-splitting distinction: how could you hate what a man did and not hate the man? But years later it occurred to me that there was one man to whom I had been doing this all my life—namely myself. However much I might dislike my own cowardice or conceit or greed, I went on loving myself. There had never been the slightest difficulty about it. In fact the very reason why I hated the things was that I loved the man. Just because I loved myself, I was sorry to find that I was the sort of man who did those things.[9]

One thing, however, is clear: We are not called to involve ourselves in the total removal of a people or nation as the sons of Israel were divinely commanded on selected occasions to do so. When the final day of the Lord comes, then God once will once again demonstrate his wrath in terrible and ominous ways. But then that will be God's option and not ours.

Discussion Questions

1. What is the difference between a "Yahweh war" and a jihad? Is this distinction contrived or does it represent real differences between the two?

2. How can God love the sinner who might be the object of a divinely authorized war and yet hate his sin enough to lead him to experience the brutality of war?

---

9. C. S. Lewis, *Mere Christianity* (New York: HarperCollins Publishers, 1980), 117.

3. How does the concept of the Hebrew word *herem* explain a story like the story of Achan and the city of Ai? What is the difference between an involuntary and a voluntary dedication or presentation of our total selves to the Lord?

4. Why was Israel prevented by the Lord from aggressively seizing territory outside the land of promise? Why was the issue different within the land of Canaan?

5. Discussion: In what ways is God waiting today for the "cup of iniquity" to be filled up for the nations of the earth? Why does God seem to take such a long time to act when evil seems to be so rampant? Will his judgment be the same for a so-called Christian nation as it will be for a non-Christian nation?

3

The God of Truth or the
God of Deception?

Question: *Is the God of the Old Testament the God
of truth or the God of deception?*

The Old Testament presents God as a God of truth, for "All [his] words are true" (Ps. 119:160), as well his "commands are true" (Ps. 119:151), and his "law is true" (Ps. 119:142). In fact, "God is not a man, that he should lie, nor a son of man, that he should change his mind" (Num. 23:19). First Samuel 15:29 also agrees with this description: "He who is the Glory of Israel does not lie or change his mind; for he is not a man, that he should change his mind."

Despite such strong assertions, in the view of some, God appears to lie or at least authorize on some occasions some type of deception. The most debated passage is probably 1 Kings 22, where the godly prophet Micaiah says that the Lord permitted a "lying spirit to enter into the mouths of all [Ahab's] prophets. [Thus] "the LORD directed disaster for [Ahab]" (1 Kings 22:23). Yet, in light of this account, and others, such as can be found in Ezekiel 14:9 (where it says, "And if a prophet is enticed to utter a prophecy, I the LORD have enticed that prophet"), some have insisted that God does on occasion lie and that he deceives others to do the same from time to time.[1] Is this an accurate reading of the text of Scripture?

---

1. J. J. M. Roberts, "Does God Lie: Divine Deceit as a Theological Problem in Israelite Literature," in *Congress Volume: Jerusalem*, VT Suppl. 40, ed. John Adney Emerton (1988), 211–20.

Walter Brueggemann is one who levels this accusation against the Lord. He states, "Yahweh here [in 1 Kings 22] obviously exercises no covenantal self-restraint, but is determined to have Yahweh's own way no matter what the cost, even if it means deceptive violence."[2] Robert P. Carroll joins in with the same accusation:

> What makes the Bible so problematic for theology is the representation in some of its narratives of Yahweh as a being who uses lies or encourages deception in order to get his own way. . . . In the story of Micaiah ben Imlah's vision . . . [t]here is a prime example of Yahweh's involvement with lies. . . . I suppose a desperate theologian might want to make subtle distinctions between encouraging others to lie and lying oneself, but both practices seem to be on the wrong side of truth-telling. [3]

No matter how it is presented, however, lying and deception are both condemned by the law of God. It would be impossible to say that God was just and truthful if he not only tempted others to sin by deceiving his creatures, but then punished the one who had carried out what was perceived to be his divine will by deceiving others. But if God cannot lie or deceive, how can these examples be understood, much less explained?

Definition of Deception

Deception or lying is the act of deluding or misleading others, regardless of the reason. It is an act condemned by Scripture. Exodus 20:16 warns, "You shall not give false testimony against your neighbor."

Such a definition immediately raises a question about the report of the midwives to Pharaoh. In response to king's plan to reduce the number of potential Hebrew soldiers for a possible uprising instigated by an enlarged number of Jewish men born to the enslaved people of Israel, the women lied to Pharaoh. Pharaoh had ordered the midwives to kill every newborn male child as they assisted the Hebrew women in childbirth (Exod. 1:15–16). However, when they reported to Pharaoh later, they explained that the reason that the male Jew-

---

2. Walter Brueggemann, *Theology of the Old Testament: Testimony, Dispute, Advocacy* (Minneapolis: Fortress, 1997), 360–62.
3. Robert P. Carroll, *Wolf in the Sheepfold: The Bible as a Problem for Christianity* (London: SPCK, 1991), 43–44.

ish birthrate was continuing to increase was due to the fact that these Hebrew women were "vigorous" and that they gave birth before the midwife could come to help them (Exod. 1:19). The truth, however, is that these women were lying for they actually "feared God," and therefore allowed the boys to live under the pretense of their not arriving on time to kill the male babies at birth.

Why then, it will be asked, did God later reward these midwives if he also disapproved of lying? Was not this a case of his rewarding these families of the midwives and therefore giving a tacit approval of their deceptions? Was this not a case where there was a conflict of two divine absolutes: 1) they should not lie, and 2) they should not murder?

No, it was not an approval of their lying or deceiving Pharaoh that is indicated in the biblical narrative, for approval of one area of a person's life is not thereby an approval of all areas of that person's life. God rewarded them because they feared him and regarded life as sacred—it was more about the fact that they feared God more than they feared the Pharaoh of Egypt. Yes, the midwives were heroes, but this is not a blanket approval of every aspect of their actions and lives. Their lying to save lives should not command our respect, nor was it meant to become something we should imitate in our lives.

Another example (but incorrectly labeled concept) of "righteous deception," according to some, is to be found in the story of Rahab (Josh. 1–2). She did indeed aid the two Hebrew spies who were trying to learn the lay of the land for the upcoming conquest of Canaan by Israel, but she also told a bald-faced lie when she answered the king of Jericho's question by saying, "Where the men went I do not know" (Josh. 2:5). She, along with her whole household, was rewarded by God with lifelong membership in Israel, but again it was not for her lying that she received God's approval. It was that she feared the God of Israel more than she feared the king of Jericho. Of course she also was also treated as a hero in the New Testament, but that was for her faith, and not for her lies that she was commended (Heb. 11:31; James 2:25). Again, approval in one area is not a *carte blanche* approval for all areas or actions in a person's life.

Truth Defined by the Philosophers

From the very inception of ethical discourse in the early Greek philosophers, a divided opinion has been observed on the question of "truth." Socrates and Plato argued that truth was determined by the gods and was therefore inviolable. Aristotle, on the other hand, argued that truth should be determined by the end results that came from an act. This has led ever since to two separate streams of thought on the truth question: "deontology," i.e., the ethics of obligation and duty as judged, for example, by the law of God; and "teleology," which relies on demonstrating what a person should do as determined by the results or consequences of their actions.[4]

On the other hand, Immanuel Kant argued that anyone who claimed to be ethical had to speak the truth without exception. This was a moral obligation in all instances; e.g., when some lied to achieve a good result or when they lied to avoid an evil, it was still a wrong. If the lying was done either to bring about good consequence or to avoid an evil result, they both were evils that should be avoided. His view illustrated the deontological point of view, but the view he opposed, as seen in his illustration, was a teleological point of view. Deontology placed duty and obligation to the truth as uppermost before trying to access its results or consequences.

In the mid-twentieth century, Dietrich Bonhoeffer took the opposite point of view. In his view it was the end result that determined if the choice was right and good. Thus, if the end result saved lives—which in his case involved plotting the murder of Adolph Hitler—then deception or lying was permitted. This illustrated the teleological view. It placed results and outcomes as having the higher priorities.

The Standard of Truth[5]

The basic Old Testament word for "truth," along with kindred word "faithfulness," is derived from a Hebrew stem from which we also get our English word "amen." The basic meaning of this Hebrew stem or root is "to be steady" or "to be firm." Even though this Hebrew word is not always rendered as "truth" in all the versions, but more often as "faithfulness," it is the opposite of falsity or falsehood. Luther, however, consistently distinguished between these two nouns in his German translation, rendering "fidelity" or "faithfulness" as *treue* and "truth" by *Wahrheit*.

Others have argued that "reliability" is a better rendering for this Hebrew word for it speaks more directly to the concepts of stability, solidarity, and firmness. These values could be seen as they were applied to the names of the col-

4. Joel E. Trull. "Deception," in *Dictionary of Scripture and Ethics*, ed. Joel B. Green (Grand Rapids: MI: Baker, 2011), 211.
5. See Henri Blocher, "The Biblical Concept of Truth," tr. H. O. J. Brown, *Themelios* 5 (1969): 47–61; John Murray, *Principles of Conduct*. (Grand Rapids, MI: Eerdmans, 1957) 131–32; M. E. Andrew, "Falsehood and Truth," *Interpretation* 17 (1963): 425–28.

umns of the temple (as "stable, solid and firm" in 2 Kings 18:16), but when "truth" was connected to "the word of God," Scripture taught that men and women were to "speak truth one to another" (Zech. 8:16). This relation of truth to words, and especially to the word of God, was the primary focus of the word "truth" in the Old Testament.

But "truth" could also be related to the *character* of persons, as in "persons of truth," i.e., persons characterized by integrity and reliability (Exod. 18:21; Deut. 1:13; Neh. 7:2). It was used also to characterize the behavior of mortals, "to do the truth, or even to "walk in the truth" (Ps. 86:11; cf. Ps. 25:5; 43:3), which depicted a whole person's lifestyle and character of a person.

The standard for truth is God himself for he is called the "God of truth" (Isa. 65:16), which can be literally rendered as "the God of amen." This attribute of truth is ascribed to him as the "God of truth" in Psalm 146:6 and Jeremiah 10:10. Moreover, God's speech is "trustworthy" (2 Sam. 7:28).

Old Testament truth ties together personality and objectivity. It relates to the facts and also to the principles. Leviticus 19:11 warns, "Do not lie," while Proverbs 6:16–19 includes a "lying tongue" as one of the seven things God "hates." "The LORD detests lying lips." Proverbs 12:22 teaches that "truthful lips endure forever" (Prov. 12:19). So harmful was the potential of a lying tongue that David dedicated one of his eight fugitive psalms, Psalm 52, to a discussion of the improper use of the tongue. Doeg the Edomite had disclosed to Saul what he thought had happened when the priest gave David's men bread and gave David Goliath's sword. Doeg had used his tongue in an improper way to tell what he was not full party to. In so doing, Doeg caused the death of some eighty priests when Saul took his vengeance.

Interestingly, the Greek word for truth, *alethia,* is composed of the alpha privative *a* on the front of the word (meaning "not") and the verb *lanthano,* "to see" (from Lethe, the river of forgetting). Thus the Greek form of *truth* might suggest the state of "not seeing." But in this Greek form, truth was impersonal. In the Old Testament, however, truth was internalized in the speaker. For example, Joseph demanded that his brothers produce Benjamin so that he might know that the truth was "in them" (Gen. 42:16).

What Constitutes a Lie?

Almost three hundred years ago, Ezekiel Hopkins (in 1701), following St. Augustine, gave this definition of a lie: "A lie . . . is a voluntary speaking of an untruth with an intent to deceive." This definition identifies three ingredients of a lie:

1. It involved the speaking of an untruth;
2. It was known to be an untruth; and
3. It involved the will and intent of the speaker to deceive and to lead the hearer into error as a result of hearing this untruth.[6]

Asa Mahan in 1840, however, sharpened this definition of a lie by making the following qualifications on the preceding definition:

1. The deception must be intentional;
2. The deceived person must have a claim or right to know the truth; and
3. Lying must be distinguished from concealing a thing, for concealment is only a sin when there is an obligation to reveal what is concealed.[7]

These qualifications are important for there are times in which concealment must be used without it being regarded as a moral evil. What must be revealed is only that which a person has a right to know. Accordingly, prophecy is one area where it is proper for our Lord to withhold part of the truth. At other times, concealment is used for the moment when a certain type of drawing-out of the person being engaged is desired. Thus, our Lord was not practicing dissimulation when he talked to the disciples on the road to Emmaus and asked, "What things?" (Luke 24:13–34). By asking the question in this way, Jesus did not intend to say that he had no idea of what was going on in Jerusalem at that time, but he wanted to know how perceptive these disciples were. Thus, he drew them out with his question.

Concealment is demanded when the person being addressed has no moral right to know the truth. That was the position of Saul in 1 Samuel 16:1–3. The prophet Samuel had been told to "fill [his] horn with oil and go on [his] way" to anoint David as king, even while Saul was still in office as king. But the prophet's question was, "How can I go? Saul will hear about it and kill me." The Lord said, "Take a heifer with you and say, 'I have come to sacrifice to the LORD'" (1 Sam. 16:1–2). Saul had no moral right to know what Samuel was up to in this situation, so the concealment was justified. But neither did Samuel have any blanket

---

6. Ezekiel Hopkins. "Exposition of the Ten Commandments," in *The Whole Works of Ezekiel Hopkins* (1701; reprint Edinburgh: A & C. Black, 1841), 134.
7. Asa Mahan, *Abstract of a Course of Lectures on Mental and Moral Philosophy* (Oberlin, OH: James Steel, 1840), 285. This was pointed out to me in 1979 by Rick Heyn, then a student at a series of visiting lectures at Belhaven College.

right to tell a falsehood, just as Saul did not have an unlimited right to know completely what was going on, due to his moral lapses in the office of king.

Mahan was asked if an intentional deception was ever allowed. His answer was:

> . . . if there is any being who has no claims upon us to receive from us the truth if he receives anything, to deceive such a being is no sin. If a man was pursued by a tiger or boa constrictor, and he should escape from it by deceiving it, all would say that he had not sinned. . . . To deceive a human being in a similar relation for self-preservation would not be sin.[8]

A Case Study: King Ahab and the Prophet Micaiah (1 Kings 22)

At first, it would appear that the Old Testament presents the God of truth as the sponsor of some type of falsehood, often inspiring prophets with false messages. One such case appears in Jeremiah 4:10. "Then I [Jeremiah] said, 'Ah Sovereign LORD, how completely you have deceived this people and Jerusalem by saying, You will have peace, when the sword is at our throats.'"

Jeremiah began by asserting God's sovereignty over everything as the baseline from which he perceived the situation, but then he proceeded to speak emphatically (using the Hebrew *hiphil* infinitive absolute, a causative form) that God has completely deceived the people and the city of Jerusalem. To be sure, God had prophesied a century earlier that when the Assyrians had threatened to invade the land (Isa. 37:33–5) that there would be peace rather than war. But it was a jump in logic to argue on the basis of conditions one hundred years or more earlier that those same conditions and results applied in this later date! These were different times and different folks; they demanded different strokes! More than that, the people also had changed drastically in their practice of righteousness and godliness. Jeremiah could also be using the literary device of irony!

In a similar way, the text of Ezekiel 14:9–11 must be understood:

> And if the prophet is enticed to utter a prophecy, I the LORD have enticed that prophet, and I will stretch out my hand against him and destroy him from among my people Israel.

---

8. Mahan, *Moral Philosophy*, 289.

They will bear their guilt—the prophet will be as guilty as the one who consults him. Then the people of Israel will no longer stray from me, nor will they defile themselves anymore with all their sins. They will be my people, and I will be their God, declares the Sovereign LORD.

It is a well-known characteristic of popular expressions to use the imperatival and active form of expressing a concept when what is understood only *permits* what appeared otherwise to be a command. For example, when our Lord heard the devils begging him to be cast into the swine instead of roaming around in the outside world after they had resided so long in the body of the demoniac, our Lord commanded them to "Go!" (Matt. 8:31). But in so saying this, he did nothing more than *permit* them to go. Likewise, when John records that Jesus commanded Judas at the Last Supper, "What you are about to do, do quickly" (John 13:27), John does not thereby intend to say that Christ authored his own betrayal. The order was a word of permission, not a direct sponsorship of the wrong and evil done.

This brings us to our key problem, the deception of the some four hundred prophets loyal to King Ahab of Israel in 1 Kings 22:2–23. King Ahab had been joined by the good but easily duped King Jehoshaphat of Judea who was asked by Ahab, "Will you go with me and fight against Ramoth Gilead?" (22:4a). As was typical of Jehoshaphat, he had the unfortunate habit of speaking first and thinking later: "I am as you are, my people as your people, my horses as your horses" (22:4b). But then he had a question for King Ahab: "I wonder what a prophet of Yahweh would say about such a move?"

To confirm the decision, King Ahab had already brought out some four hundred prophets and put the question to them: "Shall I go up to Ramoth Gilead, or shall I refrain?" (22:6b). They were all in favor of going up to fight against the city that Israel had lost years before in a previous war. But Jehoshaphat had a late arousal of conscience and asked if King Ahab had, perchance, a prophet of Yahweh around with whom he could, presumably, check the word of these four hundred-plus prophets? (22:7).

Yes, came the answer—there was Micaiah the prophet, son of Imlah, but Ahab frankly told Jehoshaphat that he hated him since he "never prophesied anything good about [Ahab]" (22:8). Currently he was in the Israelite prison of king Ahab! Jehoshaphat mildly rebuked the king and nevertheless asked for Micaiah's input (22:8c, 9).

Micaiah, having been tipped off by the summoning messenger as to how the vote was going (already the vote was four hundred to zero in favor of going to battle), and what would be best for his health by way of answers he might give, Micaiah must have sarcastically cast his message to the kings: "Attack and be victorious" (22:15c). His response seems to drip with irony and sarcastic approval! Ahab must have picked up the mocking tone of his voice for he pretended to rebuke him in a pious manner about how many times must he warn him "to speak only in the name of the Lord" (22:16) for Micaiah had been most careful not to say, "Thus says the Lord, 'Attack and be victorious.'" It is true Micaiah had said that he would only speak what the Lord told him (22:14). Thus, the absence of this most important formula, "Thus says the Lord," was not an oversight on his part; it was deliberate. Micaiah, then, seemed to switch gears and began to prophesy judgment on Ahab in his prophetic role as shepherd of the people (22:17, 19–23, 25, 28). Ahab would not make it out of that battle alive.

So how do we explain this shift in message? Which of the two messages was true? Which message came from the Lord?

One very facile, but improbable, interpretation argues that Micaiah lied because he shrank in front of such an awesome scene produced by two sitting kings from two countries surrounded by all their courtiers in a solemn display. But that explanation does not fit a prophet who was already in jail for not pulling his punches in his previous warnings to the king, and also from the fact that he went on to confront the king for his evil once again and declare judgment against him (22:19).

Others have not been any more helpful in their alternative explanations either.[9] They argued that Micaiah ben Imlah was commanded by God to tell a lie to try to stop Ahab who was already doomed to die. But this argument attributes to God a characteristic that Scripture decidedly opposed. Simon J. DeVries took another improper tack: He saw Micaiah's first prediction as a "preliminary message expressive of a patriotic strain in his ideology."[10] But this prophet does not appear to be one concerned about his popularity ratings or his level of patriotism.

---

9. Alan J. Hauser, "Should Ahab Go to Battle or Not? Ambiguity as a Rhetorical Device in 1 Kings 22," in *Rhetorical Argumentation in Biblical Texts: Essays from Lund 2000 Conference*, ed. Andeers Eriksson et al., (Harrisburg, PA: Trinity Press International, 2002), 147–48. Also Jefferies M. Hamilton, "Caught in the Nets of Prophecy? The Death of King Ahab and the Character of God," *Catholic Biblical Quarterly* 56 (1994): 654.

10. Simon J. DeVries, *I Kings: Word Biblical Commentary* (Waco, TX: Word Books, 1985), 268. Also see Peter J. Williams, "Lying Spirits Sent by God? The Case of Micaiah's Prophecy," in *The Trustworthiness of God: Perspectives on the Nature of Scripture*, ed. Paul Helm and Carl R. Trueman (Grand Rapids: Eerdmans, 2002), 62.

So what is the solution to this problem? The four hundred prophets had indeed spoken out of their own minds. If God had been trying to entrap Ahab into a life-threatening situation, he certainly would not have later have told him what he was doing and going to continue to do. Instead, because Ahab had abandoned the Lord God and hardened his own heart against the word of God, God had allowed his ruin by the very instrument Ahab had sought to prostitute for his own purposes, namely by prophecy. God would use the false declarations of the false prophets that Ahab was so enamored with as his very instrument of judgment.

Therefore, Micaiah's first prophecy was one given ironically and sarcastically, but not in any way attributed to the sure and definite word from the Lord. His second word, however, was a word of judgment, and that one would prove to be a true word from the Lord as indicated by the prophetic formula of "Thus says Yahweh."

The fact that God was able to overrule the evil Ahab had intended did not excuse the guilty prophets or their beguiled listeners. The fact that a deception was permitted did not excuse the prophets who placed their gifts at the wishes of the king. Thus the four-hundred-plus prophets and the king were alike guilty for their failure to heed the word of the Lord from the lips of Micaiah ben Imlah.

The other two passages that charge God with falsehood and deception (Jer. 4:10; 20:7; Ezek. 14:9) are answered in a similar way. In the Ezekiel passage, God allows spiritual blindness to take its course. The whole process of the hardening the heart followed by judgment is all within the sovereign will of God. In the case of Jeremiah 20:7, the prophet mistook the promise of God's presence for the assurance that he would not face derision or evil as a result of his ministry. But these instances do not amount to a charge against God's integrity or reliability.

Finally, one might also attempt to cite Judges 9:23 as one more example of God sponsoring evil. One of the judges, Gideon's son Abimelech, acted as king for three years over the city of Shechem, where he and the people were summarily sent an evil spirit from God as the citizens of Shechem "acted treacherously against Abimelech." But under the direction of divine providence, the "evil spirit" was a breaking out of discord and treachery against Abimelech, which God had allowed jealousies to arise, which subsequently turned into an insurrection, civil disorder, and ultimately bloodshed and the lose of the kingship for Abimelech. But even here, God remained in charge as he allowed what was deservedly happening to transpire without losing control of the situation or the future.

Conclusion

All God's ways and words are true. He has been, now is, and will be faithful in the future. God is not a man that he should change his mind (Num. 23:19; 1 Sam. 15:29).

At the same time, nothing, but nothing happens on earth, but that God is not still sovereign over all that takes place. If God does not actually direct any of these events, he still must permit or allow them to come to pass for his own name's sake. He is Lord over all.

Discussion Questions

1. In light of this chapter, how would you define a lie? What are the essential parts of your definition if it is to fit biblical usage?

2. How committed to the truth is God? How then does the Bible define truth?

3. If deception is the act of deluding or misleading others away from the truth, then are such acts ever permitted within the will and providence of God? Is there any difference in misleading individuals when one is playing a sport or part of an army? When I am told in the huddle that I must fake an end run to the right, should I say "I can't do that for I am an evangelical Christian; give me the ball or nothing; I can't risk my testimony"?

4. Did the midwives lie to Pharaoh and did Rahab lie to the king of Jericho? If so, is the fact that God blessed all of them an indication that it is sometimes permissible to lie?

5. How could a God of truth be involved with the lies of King Ahab's four hundred false prophets?

4

The God of Evolution or the
God of Creation?

Question: *Is the God of the Old Testament the God
of creation or the God of evolution?*

The first verse of the Bible has a memorable and distinct sentence that asserts an absolute beginning for the universe: "In the beginning [major pause, according to the Hebrew disjunctive accent], God created the heavens and the earth." No further details are given as to when this beginning occurred, or even how quickly it was connected to the narration of events that followed in verses 1:2–2:3. It is simply stated that the heavens and the earth had a definite and an absolute "beginning" in space and time; but this, of course, leads to further questions and analyses. For example:

Should Genesis 1:1 be interpreted as an independent clause ("In the beginning God created the heavens and the earth"), or should it be rendered as a dependent clause as some modern translations render it: "When God began to create . . . [t]hen he said, 'Let there be light'"? (Some translators take this approach, claiming that it is based on alleged Near Eastern parallels.)

Several recent translations (NEB, NABS, NJPS, RSV, AB), follow the opening line in the Babylonian Creation Epic, called the *Enuma Elish* (a second millennium BC Near Eastern myth assumed to be a literary parallel) which begins, "When above, the heavens had not been named, [and] below, the earth had not been called by named. . . ." These interpreters have opted for a dependent clause translation to Genesis 1:1 with the clauses in verses 1 and 2 being subordinated to the main clause, which finally came in verse 3 in Genesis 1, "Then God said. . . ."

But against such a dependent clause translation for verses 1–2 stands these facts:

1. All the ancient versions of the Bible translate the first word of Genesis as an absolute noun, "In the beginning," and understand that the first verse is an independent clause.
2. The Jewish Masoretes (scribe-scholars) of the fifth and sixth centuries AD also took the word to be an absolute for they accented the word with a disjunctive accent called a *tipchah,* rather than a conjunctive accent, meaning it was to be treated as an independent clause.
3. Isaiah 46:10 also shows the Hebrew word *reʾshit* used in the absolute sense and without an expressed article, therefore being an exact parallel to Genesis 1:1.
4. The creation literature of the ancient Near East does not come close to matching the concepts, words and descriptions of Genesis 1, as has been brilliantly argued in the past by the late University of Chicago Professor A. Heidel.[1]

Therefore, the translation, "In *the* beginning" is the way that this verse should be rendered. If this reasoning is correct, then instead of viewing the heavens and the earth as coming into being initially over a long period of time, it argues instead for a sudden bursting on the scene of the initial work of God as the very start of everything: a big bang, if you please.

But how extensive was this work of God? How much of our world was included in this appearance of physical things? The best answer is to notice that the Hebrew text does not have a word such as our English word for "universe." Instead, the words coming at the end of verse 1 are best understood as a figure of speech known as "hendiadys," where one single concept (in this case in English) is expressed by two words joined by a conjunction; therefore, the expression "heavens and earth" or the "sky and land," meant the whole cosmic "universe." God created it all! Accordingly, the first teaching block is Genesis 1:1–2:3, where the Masoretes also put an end-of-a-section marker.

This first sentence in Genesis 1:1 is also marked by the presence of the Hebrew verb, *baraʾ*, "to create." It is called a "perfect tense" in Hebrew (usually signifying a

---

1. Alexander Heidel, *Babylonian Genesis,* 2nd ed. (Chicago: University of Chicago Press, 1963).

completed action), which is not the normal narrative prose Hebrew verb form. As such, it tends to stand alone and somewhat outside the main sequence of the continuous creative activity that follows in verses 1:3–2:3.[2] It either summarizes the entire teaching block, or it describes the conditions that were present as God ordered things into existence in preparation for the first day, i.e., a work "under construction."

The verb *bara`* appears some forty-five times in the Hebrew Bible and always has "God" as its exclusive subject and is never used with any agency of material. This is as close as we can come in human language for "creat[ing something] out of nothing" (Latin: *creatio ex nihilo*), but, of course, we mortals have no call for such a term in our vocabulary since we are incapable of replicating such an act by creating something out of nothing. However, the use of *bara`* is the best human language can do for the needed unique word; or, if it is put in a more periphrastic way, Hebrews 11:3 will answer that linguistic need for a "creation out of nothing" by saying, "By faith we understand that the universe was formed at God's command, so that what is seen was not made out of what is visible."

In the apocryphal Jewish book of 2 Maccabees 7:28–29 (a non-canonical book, but a true representation of the Jewish understanding on the subject), a mother encourages each of her sons to remain steadfast as the Greek conqueror of Judea, Antiochus Epiphanes IV, martyrs them one by one. She encourages each one to not let this dictator think he can end their lives. To one she said: "I beseech thee, my son, look upon heaven and earth, and all that is in them: and consider that God made them out of nothing, and mankind also: So thou shalt not fear this tormentor."[3] This type of language reflects the same sentiments as Hebrews 11:3. God created all that is now seen, for he made it out of nothing— "By faith we understand that the universe was formed at God's command, so that what is seen was not made out of what was visible.

Formless, Empty, and Dark—Genesis 1:2

All of a sudden, however, we move from a summarizing or preparatory work of God to what could be regarded as a very dark picture. How could this be? How could what appears to be such a negative description of the state of the earth in verse 2 follow such a majestic announcement of God's absolute overall

---

2. See the fine discussion by C. John Collins. *Genesis 1-4: A Linguistic, Literary, and Theological Commentary* (Phillipsburg, NJ: P&R Publishing, 2006), 50–55.
3. Second Maccabees 7:28–29, Douay-Rheims, 1889, https://www.biblegateway.com/passage/?search=2+Maccabees+ 7%3A28-29&version=DRA (accessed March 6, 2015).

creation in verse 1? Is there not some dissonance here or at least a mid-point description in the on-going stages of the work of creation?

"Now the earth was formless and empty, darkness was over the surface of the deep, and the Spirit of God was hovering over the waters," (vs. 2).

Does not the record sound strange and out of sequence with verse 1? Suddenly the radiance and splendor of verse 1 appears to have turned empty and bleak. Moreover, it seems that even prior to the Fall of Adam and Eve there must have been a celestial and a terrestrial disturbance of some kind in God's world—perhaps one in which Lucifer, along with other angelic beings (Jude 6; 2 Peter 2:4), revolted in heaven and were cast out of that realm (Isa. 14:12–17; Ezek. 28:11–19) to the earth (a view held by some biblical scholars). Surely, all must have noticed by now that Lucifer (also named Satan but here called in Hebrew *han-nahash*, "the Serpent") was *already* in the Garden of Eden as a tempter to the first couple, Adam and Eve. Therefore, evil was somehow already present in this world, but God waited to see what the man and woman would do in the specially planned Garden of Eden. The serpent's name also always surprisingly appears in the Eden story with the definite article, while the book of Revelation calls him that "the great dragon," "the ancient serpent," "the devil," and "Satan" (Rev. 12:9). So isn't he out of place in such a pristine setting in the Garden of Eden?

Verse 2 begins, "Now the earth was formless and empty." (Hebrew *tohu vabohu*), indicating something unproductive and desolate. However, Isaiah 45:18–19 clearly affirmed that Yahweh "did not create [the universe] to be empty (Hebrew *tohu*), but he formed it to be inhabited." Therefore, it would be composed especially to be inhabited, since this text flatly denies that the earth or land had been formed to be vacated or to remain desolate, and empty. But the fact that the word *tohu* is associated with "desert," "wilderness," or the like does not signal something that it is aesthetically pleasing in most respects. Would this then indicate the fact that God gave us here the first stage in his work of creation as he assembled all of matter together and then went on to perfect it, as in a generalization that will become particularized? Or, does it point to a primordial chaos that creation took as its first state of being, which was then overcome and transformed?

It is hardly this second option, for matter is not eternal nor is there any record of a preceding civilization that was judged and then reordered subsequently by God. Since the record does not say explicitly, we must leave the issue open for the moment while being aware of several possible renderings for verse 2, with preference going to the option of stating a generalization, which then becomes a particularization in the timing of God.

The Genesis story goes on: "darkness was over the surface of the deep." The creation record does not specifically indicate that God created darkness, but it does teach that God created "light" (v. 3). However, Isaiah 45:7 says, "I form light and I create darkness." Accordingly, even though Yahweh is not said to be the author of darkness in the Genesis record, his work encompassed this part of creation as well, even though "God is light and in him is no darkness at all" (1 John 1:5). Therefore even darkness owes its existence to this Creator God.

So dissonant is this second verse with verse 1 that it was fashionable for a time in the early part of the twentieth century to posit that a previous creation or civilization had once been here on earth in verse 2. Apparently this culture was divinely destroyed because of its evil, so that God had to recreate the universe all over again, thereby making the Genesis narrative a story of a re-creation. There is no direct or circumstantial evidence, however, to support this claim, called the "Gap Theory." Especially damaging for such a claim is the fact that the verb "to be" in verse 2 is translated (according to this theory) "become/became." This linguistic move can take place in many other languages for the verb "to be" but not in Hebrew. In Hebrew there is a special preposition *le*, "to," that is used with the Hebrew verb *hayay*, "to be," when it is meant to say "become/became," (i.e., "to be . . . to," *hayah le*). This form of the verb with an attached preposition does not appear in verse 2 as it does appear in Genesis 9:13 (Hebrew, *wehayetah le`ot*, "let it [the rainbow] *become* a sign*," emphasis mine). Therefore, we do not support the view that a former civilization perished as God recreated the world all over again in the rest of Genesis 1 for the text does not support this claim.

Some have held the view that the Hebrew word for "deep" (Hebrew *tehom*) was a tell-tale sign that the Babylonian goddess named Tiamat in the Babylonian *Enuma Elish* myth was one of the main characters responsible for this creation narrative (based on the similar group of words). But that suggestion has been thoroughly discredited by means of philological research on these words.[4] The difficulty with borrowing a feminine Babylonian word and then bringing it over into Hebrew (which in Hebrew has an <u>additional</u> guttural letter "h" in the middle of it) is impossible to account for morphologically. Such an equation of terms is a "complete fallacy," according to Kenneth Kitchen.[5] The Hebrew word *tehom,*

---

4.   Heidel, *Babylonian Genesis*, 119.
5.   Kenneth A. Kitchen, *Ancient Orient and the Old Testament* (Chicago: InterVarsity Press, 1966) 89–90.

"deep, depths," comes much more likely from a similar early Ugaritic word that clearly means "deep," or "ocean," not from any alleged Babylonian *tehom*.

Finally, some want to see in verse 2 "the s/Spirit/ wind of God" as a reflection of the *Enuma Elish*'s use of "mighty winds" in its story, but those winds were *evil* winds in the pagan story. However, those who try to translate this expression as if *Elohim* could be rendered as an intensifying adverb meaning a "*mighty* wind," will find it almost impossible to do so, both in this text and in the rest of the Old Testament, for *Elohim* is not used as an intensifying adverb meaning "mighty." In fact, if that is what the writer wanted to say, he could readily have used the Hebrew *ruah gedolah* ("great wind") which is used in 1 Kings 19:11; Job 1:19; and Jonah 1:4. Therefore, God's spirit, or better still, the "Spirit of God," hovered over the waters as he superintended their boundaries, limits, and purposes.

Let There Be Light—Genesis 1:3–5

The opening story of the Bible describes how, in six steps, God the Creator made the world and everything in it, followed by his rest from all his work on the Sabbath. If verses 1–2 spoke of the initial acts of creation as things got underway before day 1, then verse 3 actually begins the *wayyiqqtol* sequence, which is the Hebrew grammar's signal of the normal narrative prose genre that moved the story forward in the sequence of the events God initiated.

On this first "day" God ordered the appearance of "light." But if day and night are marked off by the two great lights (later known as the sun and the moon and made on the fourth day), how was it possible, St. Augustine observed to have "days and nights" marked off on the first three "days"? Was the light mentioned in verse 3 provided through some other means than the sun and the moon, or is this a textual clue that the word "day" is being used in this context in another way than what one would immediately and naturally presume, that is until they had studied the passage more closely?

In fact, the word "day" (Hebrew, *yom*) is used three different ways in this very same passage:

1. verse 5 where God calls the light "day"
2. verse 14 where God marks off "days" by using the greater (the sun) and the lesser light (the moon) to "serve as signs to mark the seasons, days and years"
3. in 2:4 summarizing all seven creative "days"

The writer concludes, "This is the account of the heavens and the earth *in the day* when they were created" (my translation). Moreover, the same author of this part of the book of the law, Moses, says in Psalm 90:4 that "A thousand years in your sight are like a day that has just gone by."

Some have tried to get around this problem by saying the words of verse 3 do not demand that God created "light" (Hebrew, `or) on that first creative work period (note that the singular for "light" is used), but that he actually made the "lights" (Hebrew plural, me`orot) later in 1:16 (note the plural). But this reading of the text requires a good deal of imputed imagination, for where, then, did the light come from? However, no separate source for this light of verse 3 is suggested in the text. Others theorize that as the atmosphere began to clear, a general light from the universe itself was what God appointed on the first day, apart from the creation of the sun and moon on the fourth day, which later also gave off light on that "day" four. However, it is impossible to say definitively that this is the correct interpretation.

The structure of the refrain for these six "days" must be noted for they conclude each day's work using the same expression: "And there was evening and there was morning, the first day." But the Hebrew order of the words is also important; it is evening followed by morning. The most striking observation that must be made here is that such phrasing is not a complete definition for what is ordinarily meant by our usage of the word "day." If one is going to demand such here, then that will run counter to the writer's own use of his terms. To put it more bluntly, evening and morning bracket a "night" time, but seems it fails to embrace the afternoon as part of that "day" time with that night. The Hebrew makes it clear that there are successive events, each designated by "and there was" or "it came to pass."

Unfortunately, the Authorized Version (KJV) puts the two events into one: "And the evening and the morning were the first day." However, the text says "And there was evening and there was morning, the first day." Thus, they fix two opposite points of a nighttime, but not the limits for what we call "day." Thus, the refrain, "and there was evening, and there was morning, the n-th day" functions as a good colophon for each act of creation, marking each creative act off as being distinctive and concluding that work period. But it hardly seems interested in delimiting the amount of time that had expired for that creative act.

Let There Be an Expanse—Genesis 1:6–8

On the second work "day," God spoke again and ordered that there should be an "expanse" (Hebrew, *raqia*), which comes from the Hebrew root "to beat out," "to spread out," or even "an expanse," but certainly not the idea conveyed by the Latin Vulgate rendering of a "firmament" (or the Greek Septuagint rendering *stereoma*), as if it were some sort of solid dome that stretched over the earth, much like a sports stadium's solid dome spreads over the field of play. This "expanse" separated the water under this expanse from the water of the clouds above the expanse.

The Hebrew word *raqia'* is better rendered as an "expanse" than as a "canopy" or something "hard" or "firm" as it usually is incorrectly translated and depicted as a "firmament" in verses 7, 8, 14, 15, 17, and 20. From an empirical point of view, the idea of the sky as a dome would seem to dictate that the heavens were composed of a semi-spherical vault that was spread out to form a celestial hard ceiling with appropriate holes interspersed every so far apart to let in rain drops and the like.

But that conclusion would substitute appearances and phenomenological language for reality and the hard facts of reality—even for nature itself. It would likewise be wrong to affirm that this word pointed to some sort of "vapor canopy" that at one time spread over the earth until the first flood came with a major change in the weather pattern which then dissipated the whole picture. But that too would be speculative and unsupported by anything in the text. On balance, it is best to render the skies as an "expanse." Those who render *raqia'* as a "dome" are more influenced by Near Eastern myths than they are guided by the revelation of God.

Let the Land Produce Vegetation—Genesis 1:9–13

God ordered the dry land and the seas to appear in his third creative act. Here was another act of separation, but it also was followed by a second work on this third "day" in which the land produced vegetation and plants bearing seeds and growing vegetation, or in the case of the fruit trees, fruit with "seed in them according to their kinds."

The meaning of the word "kind" (Hebrew, *le-min*) is not to be equated automatically as our biological or botanical descriptive categorization of "species," as some incorrectly have assumed (calling for the "fixity of the species" in the creative order), for it can occasionally also be used of classifications all the way up to the biological level of "order" in the system that arbitrarily assigns 'kinds" to biological categories based on observation and purely human arrangement. Where it fails to offer help is in one those mega-moves of macro-evolution where evolutionary theory demands these mega-changes extended all the way across the classification categories to that of "classes," "phyla," or "kingdoms." Without evidence for such mega-jumps in the order of animals or plants, evolution remains an unproven speculative theory, which merely pleads for more time to allow both the observation and empirical evidence for this phenomenon.

The same Hebrew word *le-min,* "according to its kind" is used of all living creatures in 1:21, 24–25. Therefore, this is neither a technical term nor a biological professional classification, but instead it is a word indicating that each form of the seed produces the same "variety," "types," or "categories" as that which gave it birth. Beans do not come from corn seed, nor do other areas fail to remain true to its own category in the animal world as well.

Let There Be Lights in the Expanse—Genesis 1:14–19

When we come to the fourth creative act of God, we are back into the problem that was presented to us on the first work "day." Did the "light" begin on day one or on day four? But what if this problem was left in the text to help us see that the meaning of the word "day" meant something different from our ordinary understanding of the word "day?" Three work "days" have already occurred before we have had the creative markers for those "days" demarcated by the appearance of sun and the moon. No matter how much some may protest, the Bible insists that "days", were created on day four.

C. John Collins tries to get around this problem by saying that "The verb *made* in Genesis 1:16 does not specifically mean 'create.'" It can refer to that, he acknowledged, but it can also refer to "working on something that is already there."[6] Collins cites Rashi (a famous Jewish rabbi) to back up this unusual suggestion for verse 14. Rabbi Rashi claimed that God created the lights on the first day, and that on the fourth day God commanded that they be hung in the expanse. But the sun and the moon are not like so many pictures that need to be mounted and which otherwise remain spread around until they become firmly attached. Collins' point is that verse 14 focuses on the "function of the light," and not their "origin." But again, this is a chapter on *origins* and not one addressed primarily to *function,*[7] so where is the evidence

---

6. Collins. *Genesis 1–4,* 57.
7. John H. Walton, *The Lost World of Genesis One: Ancient Cosmology and the Origins Debate* (Downers Grove, IL: IVP Academic, 2009) argues for their functionality.

for function instead of origins? Therefore, the light and its source on day one must be different from the "day" inaugurated on "day" four. The problem of distinguishing between the two "lights" remains.

Let the Waters Teem and the Birds Fly—Genesis 1:20–23

God said to let the waters "swarm" or "teem" with "living creatures" (Hebrew, *nephesh hayyah*). This expression is found in Genesis 1:21, 24, 30 and 2:7, 19. It is easier to say what it means than it is to give a single succinct English term or two for this expression that fits all the varied instances noted above. The Hebrew phrase points to "an animated living being" or one that is just plain "alive." It is true that the word *nephesh* means "soul" in some contexts, but it does not appear to point in this instance to some spiritual aspect of all these creatures. Instead, it points to the fact that they are "alive" and "living." Therefore, "living creatures" is not a bad rendering for the Hebrew original at all.

Even though verse 20 renders the Hebrew *'oph* as "birds," the word simply means "flying [things]." Thus the category is wider than merely birds since it would also include such flying things as insects, bats, and the like.

On this same day God created "the great sea creatures" (Hebrew, *tannin*). Wenham in his commentary on Genesis makes these into "great sea monsters,"[8] and others have rendered the term as "giant marine animals"—as if these were some sort of mythical beasts. It is best to follow the lead of Heidel here, where he correctly argued that these were such "sea monsters" as whales and sharks.[9]

God Made Wild Animals, Livestock, Man, and Woman—Genesis 1:24–31

Each of the six creative works of God has been introduced with "And God said. . . . " But in verse 26 it adds, "Let us make man in our image." What does the word "us" in that statement refer to? To be sure, this is not an indication of an originally polytheistic account, for Scripture steadfastly resists such a thesis. It could mean, according to others, that God was speak-

---

8. Gordon J. Wenham, *World Biblical Commentary: Genesis 1-15 vol.1* (Waco, Texas: World Books,1987), 24.
9. Heidel, *Babylonian Genesis,* 104.

ing to the heavenly court of his angels, but there are no indications in the text that this is what is meant here either.

Any talk about a disclosure, an allusion to, or even an assumption here of the Trinity within the Godhead is too early for such an interpretation, according to many interpreters. However, the Spirit has already been revealed as early as verse 2. So, despite the fact that this may simply be a "plural of majesty" for the Godhead, it is difficult to entirely reject the idea that here is some indication that the God of the Bible has always been a Trinity from eternity past and always will be a Trinity.

What then is "the image of God," which is placed both within the man and the woman (1:26, 27)? The discussion of this phrase is enormous, but usually not as helpful as their enormity would suggest.

First of all, there are two terms used in this context for this attribute, which is distinctive in the human couple. Verse 26 says, "Let us make man in our image, in our likeness." The Hebrew forms for these two words are: *tselem,* "image," and *demut,* "likeness" or "resemblance"; or as they appear with different prepositions, "In the image," and "after the likeness" of God. But there does not appear to be a concerted difference between the two terms, or separate uses of their prepositions. The man and the woman are made to resemble God. But what are these resemblances like?

This resemblance is found in these areas: these mortals are to have the dominion over the rest of the created order (1:28). As "dominion-havers," they are responsible to superintend the works of God with full and final accountability to him. But also as part of this image, they will have the gift of speech, in addition to the gift of love, and from later teaching in the New Testament, we find that this image also includes "knowledge" (Col. 3:10) and "righteousness and holiness" (Eph. 4:26). A clear line of demarcation now sets the humans off from all the rest of the creative works of God. The man and the woman were meant to be distinctive and to reflect their Creator!

God Finished His Work on the Seventh Day—Genesis 2:1–3

As separate from the previous six work days of God, this "day" did not include the refrain found on the other six. But the announcement here is that God had "finished" (2:2) his work and he now "rested" (2:3). Accordingly, God "blessed" this "seventh day and made it holy" (2:3). This pattern of work and rest was provided for the man and woman made in his image. It would be a model from that time forward.

The "Sabbath," or "stop-day," was also meant to set a clear demarcation between God's work in creation and his continued work in providence. A second such "stop-day" came as he declared on the cross—"It is finished" (John 19:30)—which set a line marking off Christ's plan to bring salvation and his provision of it in his death and resurrection. A third and final "stop-day" can be seen in Revelation 21:6, where Christ announces "It is done," and a line is drawn between history and eternity.

Conclusion

1. God is the subject of virtually every action verb in this account: He creates, says, sees, separates, names, makes, finishes, and blesses. How can some incorrectly say that this is not a chapter on origins, but one that deals only with functions or with a theology of the tabernacle where God proclaims rest once again?

2. If an exception is to be found here to God's direct action in creation, Genesis 1:12 has what at first appears as a mediate and not an immediate action of our Lord as the "land [is ordered to] produce vegetation," yet even here it was in response to the command of God (1:11), which is stated in close association with what might otherwise appear to be an exception.

3. The central point of emphasis in this passage is the creation of the man and the woman in the image of God. This is the climax and high point the text wishes us to see.

4. Genesis 1:1–2:3 declares both that God is the author of creation and the method he used to create the world: He created the world by the word of his mouth. Before he spoke, the object focused on did not exist, but after he spoke there is was! The text does not allow for change to come about in other ways, such as evolutionary theories argue.

Discussion Questions

1. If no single Hebrew or English verb means "to create out of nothing," how can this meaning be established as correct?

2. If God creates all things good, what is the source of the "darkness" in Genesis 1:2 and "The Serpent" in the Garden of Eden? Is darkness always a sign of evil? Did some evil occur before the fall of Adam and Eve if Satan is already present in the Garden of Eden?

3. What is the meaning of the word "day" when used before the forming of "days" on "day four"? How is the expression "It was evening and it was morning" used in Genesis 1?

4. Does God place a "dome" over the earth, as is found in some Near Eastern myths? What is the meaning of this term in the Genesis account?

5. What does the Hebrew expression *nephesh hayah* mean when applied to the aquatic creatures and to the man and woman? (see Gen. 1:21, 24)

5

The God of Grace or
the God of Law?

Question: *Does the God of the Old Testament re-
quire that believers observe the Law or
are believers saved by his grace and
live under His grace?*

In the opinion of some, God gave his people Israel some strange laws at Sinai,
to say the least. The Torah, the first five books of the Old Testament, contains
the Mosaic Law and makes for some fascinating reading—but it also seems at
time to be excessive in its penalties, sanctions, and demands when compared to
our modern society.

For example, "Whoever curses his father or his mother must be put to
death" (Exod. 21:17). The problem here is not the principle of honoring one's
parents, but the sanction of stoning the offspring if the parental relationship
should break down. Is the death penalty the best way to handle that kind of situation? Is "stoning" really the appropriate form of punishment?

Or consider another example: An Ammonite or a Moabite must not be
allowed into the congregation of the Lord until the tenth generation (Deut.
23:3). But how does such a length of time solve anything, and what is the
reason for the long period of delay? In fact, no reason is stated in the text as to
why this is so. But surely this seems to go beyond the wide promise of blessing given to all persons and races in Genesis 12:3 (and amplified in the New
Testament in Galatians 3:29). Would not the story of Ruth have violated that

exception for she was a Moabite whose descendants were in the very line of the Messiah no less?

Another rather strange law was the prohibition of boiling a baby goat in his mother's milk (Exod. 34:26). Few contemporary believers have been tempted to apply that law in these modern days, so why was it necessary for Israel? And how did the later Jewish interpretation come about that this law was the stated basis for not simultaneously eating or mixing meat or milk products, that is, not commingling dishes that had served meat with dishes having milk (such as a cheeseburger)? But once again the biblical text provides not even one hint of an explanation as to why this rule was necessary either in those days or in the present, much less provide the grounds for separating meat and milk products and their utensils. Perhaps there was something instinctively known from the culture of that day that made the prohibition all the more obvious so that it needed no further explanation, but we have no record either way.

One more illustration will round out our examples. The Law required that a man who married a second wife had to give fair and equal treatment to the first wife's children (Exod. 21:10). What is clear in this law is the need for fairness—all can see that. But this law seems at times to also be linked to polygamy (unless the first wife had died)! How can polygamy be among those laws that seem to be tacitly approved when God established monogamy as the norm in the Garden of Eden? (Gen. 2:24). Yet, this law is just as much a law from God as any of the other ones are (Exod. 21:1), so can we now conclude that God is in favor of multiple wives? If polygamy is now approved, then what about polyandry for the wives as well? (see chapter 5 on polygamy).

So we must ask, how did the Old Testament Law function in the life of the believer in the Old Testament, and how does it continue to direct a Christian's obedience to the Law? Since times have changed, should we now say that the relevance of these laws from Moses has changed for the Christian? And what about the consistency of God's own directions and teachings on these matters as well?

If we say times have changed and therefore so has the teaching on some of these matters, did not Jesus say that he had *not* come to abolish the Law of Moses or the writings of the prophets, but he had come instead to fulfill them? In fact, Jesus warned that the whole heaven and the earth would disappear before even the smallest detail of God's Law would be rendered null and void (Matt. 5:17–20). If that is so, now what do we do? Must we now live with these incongruities?

How far does that smallest detail of Scripture inspiration extend to, the "jot and the tittle" of the Law? (Matt. 5:18). And how are we to reconcile that teaching with what the apostle Paul taught in Romans 7:4–6? There Paul taught:

> So then, dear friends, the point is this: The Law no longer holds you in its power, because you died to its power when you died with Christ on the cross. And now you are united with the one who was raised from the dead. As a result, you can produce good fruit, that is, good deeds for God. When we were controlled by our old nature, sinful desires were at work within us, and the law aroused these evil desires that produced sinful deeds, resulting in death. But now we have been released from the law, for we died with Christ, and we are no longer captive to its power. Now we can really serve God, not in the old way by obeying the letter of the law, but in the new way, by the Spirit.

So what do we do about the Law of God in light of this teaching? Should Christians be following and obeying the Mosaic Law, or have we missed something here?

As far as the Scriptures are concerned, the Law never was intended to be a heavy albatross hung around the neck of the people of Israel; instead, Moses taught, under the Lord's inspiration: "What great nation is there, that has statutes and ordinances so righteous as all this law, which I set before you this day?" (Deut. 4:8). Israel was privileged to receive the Law instead of it being a burden or grief to them! How were the people of Israel—and more importantly, how are contemporary Christians—supposed to respond to the Law of God?

Different Methods Historically of Handling Old Testament Law

History shows us various ways in which different groups have applied the Law of God in their own lives. At one extreme there is the view commonly called "Theonomy" or "Dominionism," also known as "Christian Reconstructionism." This school of thought argues that many of the Old Testament laws, and all of its penalties, are still in effect today. The name, "theonomy," is taken from the Greek words *theos* ("God") and *nomos* ("law") and means "law of God." This school of thought was at its height in the late 1970s and early 1980s.

This group took Christ's words in Matthew 5:17–20 about the "jot and title" (meaning even the most incidental features of the Law) very literally and quite directly. They applied straightforwardly all the laws from Israel's day to believers today (and to unbelievers as well), just as these laws were understood in Israel's ancient times, including the sanctions/penalties. Their hope was that the federal governments of every country in the world would enforce the Mosaic laws and penalties as a blueprint for modern society. This group did acknowledge, however, that the ceremonial laws had been fulfilled in the death and resurrection of Christ, just as Hebrews 7–10 teaches. They argued, however, that the moral law and the civil law (which they held were illustrations of the moral law in operation), along with all of their penalties, including the death penalty, were still in force today.

At the other end of the spectrum are those schools of thought called "Dispensationalists," who argued that we are, for all intents and purposes, finished with the Law. The classical form of this view is best illustrated by C. I. Scofield, who commented on Old Testament Law:

> The most obvious and striking division of the word of truth is that between Law and Grace. Indeed, these contrasting principles characterize the two most important dispensations—Jewish and Christian. . . . Scripture never, in *any* dispensation, mingles these two principles.[1]

Charles C. Ryrie, a leading dispensationalist author, made a similar point:

> [T]he Mosaic Law is done away, [but this] is not to say that there is no law in the world or that the Christian is free to live as he chooses. There are two important passages which teach that the law of Moses is done away. The first is Hebrews 7:11–12 ['For the priesthood being changed, there is made of necessity a change of the law.']. . . . And the second passage is II Corinthians 3:7–11. . . . ["Now if the ministry that brought death, which was engraved in letters on stone, came with glory, so that the Israelites could not look steadily at the face of Moses, . . . will not the ministry of the Spirit be even more glorious?][2]

---

1. C. I. Scofield, *Rightly Dividing the Word of Truth* (Findlay, OH: Fundamental Truth, 1940), 5.
2. Charles C. Ryrie, *The Grace of God* (Chicago, IL: Moody Press, 1963), 101–02.

The roots of Dispensationalism began sometime around 1830, and this view was popularized mainly through the ministry and writings of John Nelson Darby (1800–1882), the *Scofield Reference Bible* (1909), Dallas Theological Seminary, the Bible School movement in the United States and the numerous summer Bible conferences in the United States and England.

Over against both of these approaches stands Covenant Theology, which was particularly popular with Puritan and Reformed theologians of Germany and Holland, beginning in the latter part of the sixteenth and continuing through the seventeenth centuries. The concept of a covenant, of course, has extremely old roots, for it was a part of the ancient Near East for thousands of years. In order to "make a covenant," (or, as Hebrew says more literally, "to cut a covenant"), either one party or both parties would walk down an aisle formed by the animals that had been cut into two and divided in half to form that aisle, thereby the person(s) taking an oath on themselves pledged that if they did not keep the terms of the covenant, they too would end up like the split animals: dead! An example of this can be seen in Genesis 15:9–18; where, God alone passed between the divided pieces as a "smoking firepot with a blazing torch," saying in effect: May I, God, die if I do not keep what I have promised to do for Abraham and his descendants. That covenant, then, is as eternal as God himself is.

For Israel, an integral part of the covenant relationship was the Law of God, which was revealed in Moses' day. These laws did not establish that relationship, but the laws were for those who had already experienced the grace and love of God in the Old Testament. In fact, these laws gave to them direction and instruction on how to live life and to enjoy it to the fullest. One of the core texts was the Holiness Law of Leviticus 19:1, "Be holy because I the Lord your God am holy." This did not mean people were perfect and without sin as God was, but it did signal that they were "set apart and dedicated to God." Holiness also carried the idea of "wholeness," therefore one's "whole" life was to be lived in obedience to God and as a sacrifice to him: that was one's goal and aim in life.

All three views wrestled with finding a signal in Scripture that indicated what was temporal in the Law of God and what was permanent. Such a signal, however, came in the ceremonial laws concerning the tabernacle, the offerings and the festivals. For example, Moses was told in Exodus 25:9, 40 that he was to make the tabernacle "exactly like the *pattern* I will show you. . . ." Here was the large clue that this tabernacle and its sacrifices and rituals were temporary and a mere copy of the real. Whenever the real would come, as later happened in Jesus

Christ's work of the cross, the "model" or "pattern" (Hebrew *tabnit*) would be antiquated. That, of course, was the point of Hebrews 7:11–17. This meant that much of Exodus 25–40, almost all of Leviticus, and a good deal of Numbers was part of the "pattern" and therefore had a expiration date of Easter Sunday, when the real came in the death and resurrection of Jesus.

A Theological Framework of Old Testament Law

Nevertheless, the five books of the Mosaic Law still contain, apart from the ceremonial parts of the Law, a bewildering number of prescriptions ranging from rules about slavery, animals, land, and the like, to other rules governing witchcraft, leprosy, sexual conduct, and sacrifices. How are we to sort out all the topics of this enormous list and decide which ones have a continuing authority in our day as the word "pattern" of "copy" pointed to some directions that were only of temporal use?

The Ten Commandments.

God succinctly summarized the rules for living by reducing them to just ten commands (also called "the Decalogue" from a Greek word meaning "ten words" or "sayings"). These were not given as rules for being initiated or entering into the people of God, or as a basis for gaining eternal life with God forever, but they were mainly and first of all for those who already believed. These were aids for living as God had planned for his people to live. These ten laws formed the heart of the moral law of God for they reflected God's character, thus supplying a permanent norm for all of life. The Decalogue (or Ten Commandments) was known as "apodictic laws," laws that are expressed in commands and prohibitions ("thou shalt" and "thou shalt not"), and they contain the principles for godly living no matter where one lived or in what era or time setting. These laws were as durable and permeable as God is in himself, for they were based on the character of God!

Deuteronomy.

The Decalogue also forms the very structure for most of the book of Deuteronomy for there each of the ten commandments is illustrated in the same order and sequence as the ten laws, at least from Deuteronomy 12:1 to 25:16. This connection between the Decalogue and Deuteronomy was expanded to the earlier chapters of Deuteronomy as well. Other scholars have noted that Deuteronomy chapters 5–11 are moral admonitions that are an expansion of and commentary on the first commandment of the Decalogue. A chart of these chapters would look like this:

Commandment	Deuteronomy	Description
1–2	4:1–12:31	Worship
3	13:1–14:27	God's Name
4	14:28–16:17	Sabbath
5	16:18–18:22	Authority
6	19:1–22:8	Homicide
7	22:9–23:19	Adultery
8	23:20–24:7	Theft
9	24:8—25:4	False Witness
10	25:5–16	Coveting

Book of the Covenant.

Another type of laws are known as "casuistic," or "case laws" and are found in the "Book of the Covenant," the section of Exodus from 20:19 to 23:33. Their distinguishing mark is the presence of the words "if" or "when" (such and such happens), which conditional cases were then concluded with an apodosis (the clause expressing the consequence: if this, *then that*). Typically these laws took up cases involving slaves, homicides, bodily injuries, property damages, sacred seasons, and the like.

Law of Holiness.

Leviticus 18–20 is another distinct section with a formal introduction in 18:1–5 and a formal closing in 20:22–26. The phrase, "I am the LORD your God" appears nearly fifty times in these chapters, which sets out the foundational principles for sexual behavior (18), social morality (19), family worship (20:1–8, 27), and holiness in family relations (20:9–26).

Threefold Division of the Law

It was our Lord Jesus himself who made the distinction between the more important/relevant laws and those that did not have top priority, i.e., they weighted less than the other laws. Jesus taught the principle about such a hierarchy of these laws in Matthew 23:23:

"Woe to you, teachers of the law, Pharisees, you hypocrites! You tithe a tenth of your spices—mint, dill and cumin. But you have neglected the more important matters of the law—justice, mercy and faithfulness. You should have practiced the latter, without neglecting the former."

Some hold that Jesus' enumeration of "justice, mercy, and faithfulness" takes on this form: (1) justice—the moral law, which included the ten commandments (Exod. 20; Deut. 5), the holiness law (Lev. 18–20) and the book of Deuteronomy; (2) mercy—the civil law, which was made up of case laws in the Covenant Code (Exod. 20:22–23:33); and (3) faithfulness—the ceremonial laws, including all the instructions for building the tabernacle (Exod. 25–40); instructions on the sacrifices (Lev. 1–7); clean and unclean foods (Lev. 10–12); and rituals and festivals (Lev. 23–25). On this basis, only the first two forms, i.e., the moral law and the principles illustrated in the civil law, are still relevant and operative today.

A Paradigmatic Approach

But this distinction is not a satisfactory division for everyone for the categories Jesus used in Matthew 23:23 are not those directly or formally found in either the Old or New Testaments. Therefore, some look to the "Paradigmatic Approach" to distinguish what is relevant for us from the Law of God and what is no longer relevant. For example, Chris Wright defines a *paradigm* as "a model of an example for other cases where a basic principle remains unchanged, though the details differ."[3] The use of the word "paradigm" is familiar from the study of languages where one learns the various forms of the verbs in that foreign language by applying the correct form of the word to each person and number for the entire conjugation, thus forming the "paradigm."

---

3. C. J. H. Wright, *Living as the People of God: The Relevance of Old Testament Ethics* (Leicester, UK: Inter-Varsity Press, 1983), 43. Published in the USA as *An Eye for an Eye: The Place of Old Testament Ethics Today* (Downers Grove, IL: InterVarsity Press, 1983).

Thus, in Old Testament ethics, some of this group of interpreters looks at the laws paradigmatically, serving as models, as they search for the basic principles which they then try to adapt them to our own times.[4] As Wright defines his method, his use of paradigm involves identifying principles, models, and examples. Commenting on his approach, he has said,

> I wouldn't divide up the law into asking what is moral law that we must obey because that seems very reductionist. I prefer to start out with what Paul said in 2 Tim. 3:16 that all Scripture is breathed out by God and is useful for teaching, rebuking, correcting and training in righteousness. Therefore, the question is not about what is a moral law and which is not but rather to ask in what ways does a given passage claim my ethical obedience? What are the principles in it? What are the paradigms it is suggesting? What are the values, priorities in this law?[5]

For Wright, the ethical demands of the Old Testament are grounded less in laws and rules than in the character of God Himself, especially His love and justice. In his view, therefore reaching conclusions about the applicability of a particular passage involves a process of obtaining principles from the Ten Commandments and the moral laws of the Old Testament. This becomes the basis for applying the cases and illustrations found in the civil laws as well as the rest of the Torah and biblical narratives as well.

So how then do we use the Law of God correctly? Christians know that Christ's death and resurrection fulfills the Ceremonial law. We also know that the Moral Law of God is absolute and solidly based on the unchanging character of God and therefore is to be taken at face value. But what about the Civil law of God?

For interpreting and using the Civil law of God we must ask what is the *principle* that lies behind the directions given to us in Scripture. For example, Deuteronomy 25:4 teaches us: "Do not muzzle an ox while it is treading out the grain." If this were meant to be taken literally, then all who did not own a farm with oxen could feel excused from observing this Law of God. However, the *principle*

---

4. Some who use a paradigmatic model reject the idea of deriving "principles" from the text.
5. Interview with Chris Wright, King's Evangelical Divinity School https://www.kingsdivinity. org/courses/28-college/theological-articles/144-interview-with-chris-wright (accessed March 10, 2015).

remains for all to observe today. The apostle Paul used this text on two separate
occasions in 1 Corinthians 9:9 and 1 Timothy 5:18 to teach that those who are
taught the word of God should generously pay their pastors and teachers salaries
for they have worked hard to serve them. The point of Deuteronomy 25:4, then,
was that God was more interested in what happened in the life and hearts of the
owners of the oxen than he was at this moment concerned about the oxen. If the
farmer did not remove an ox's muzzle as it went round and round, trampling out
the grain from the husk, then the stinginess and hardheartedness of the farmer was
under the rebuke of God. In an *a fortiori* argument (from the lesser to the greater)
that *principle* could be seen in numerous other sectors of life. Don't be tight-fisted,
but be generous and open-handed as you share with others who minister to you
the grace that God has worked on your own heart.

Another illustration that shows how to get a *principle* from a Civil Law
comes from Deuteronomy 22:8: "When you build a new house, make a parapet
around your roof so that you may not bring guilt of bloodshed on your house if
someone falls from the roof."

Of course, most parts of the world do not build houses today with flat roofs,
but that does not mean that all of those with a pitched roof house are excused from
this law. The *principle* remains, for if some have a swimming pool in their back
yard, then they would be obligated to make sure that pool was securely fenced off
so no child or animal would fall in the pool and drown. The rule, therefore, for
interpreting the Civil Law of God is that the interpreter should seek to *principlize*
these laws rather than to expect that they should be interpreted literally.

God's Law as a Gracious Gift

We have already seen that Moses and the people of Israel did not find God's
Law strange, outlandish, or irrelevant, as some do today; rather, they regarded
themselves as privileged to have received so righteous a set of statutes and ordinances (Deut. 4:8). In fact, the very context of the Ten Commandments was
that of *grace*, for that is how the Decalogue begins in Exodus 20:2: "I am the
Lᴏʀᴅ your God, who brought you out of Egypt, out of the land of slavery."
Surely that indicates that the environment of the Law was grace! This is my preferred model for understanding the Law.

It is all too easy today to see the Law as an irritant, something one must do
or perform. On the positive side, however, the apostle Paul concluded, "The commandment is holy, just and good" (Rom. 7:12), for "I agree that the law is good"

(Rom. 7:16), and "I delight in the law of God, in my inmost being (Rom. 7:22). Of course, 1 Timothy 1:8–11 taught that the law is for the disobedient, rather than for the obedient, but the Law does point out our sin for all of us (Rom. 7:7; 4:15). But it also gives us the path for those who already believe that we should walk in it.

Jesus himself set a good model when he used the Law as the basis for principled behavior. He was not an opponent to the Law, but rather he was the Law's defender (Matt. 5:17–20). However, our Lord had little time for those who focused on the externals in keeping the Law (as those who gave priority to the Jewish *oral* traditions as in "You have heard it said") without any response to the internal call made in that same Law. If love was missing, the very Law of God itself was probably in jeopardy as well. This is exactly the charge Jesus leveled against many Jewish people of his day: they kept the externals of the Law but left off keeping the Law and their hearts clean as well. Jeremiah 7:4 made the same charge: the people rallied to the mantra of "The Temple of the Lord, the Temple of the Lord, the Temple of the Lord," but they neglected many of the other matters of the Law that began with the heart.

Nowhere else did the issue of the Law come to a greater point of debate than at the Jerusalem Council in Acts 15. There the Christian community wrestled with the problem of the Law, trying to determine which of the commands of God were still valid for believers who were not Jewish. They knew that the prophet Jeremiah had promised in the New Covenant (Jer. 31:31–34) that a day was coming when the Law itself would be written on the human heart and not just on stone; then the human heart and the divine will would be in sync.

The reason for this heart implantation was easy to see for just as a tradesman depends less and less on manuals as he gains more and more experience in carrying out his trade, so believers who have increased in maturity have less and less need for specific instructions in all they do as Christians.

It is true, of course, that God does not change—Malachi 3:6 says, "For I the Lord do not change." This statement, however, refers to his character, nature, attributes, and his covenantal faithfulness, not to the laws he has given. He remains consistent in himself although he can change in his actions depending on the needs of humans, while remaining unchanging in his very nature and being.

For example, Deuteronomy 23:1 clearly teaches: "No one who has been emasculated by crushing or cutting may enter the assembly of the Lord." This command concerning eunuchs seems to be unequivocal; only those who were complete, intact males could belong to the community of God. But what shall we make of Isaiah 56:3–5?

> Let no foreigner who has bound himself to the LORD say, "The LORD will surely exclude me from his people." And let not any eunuch complain, "I am only a dry tree." For this is what the LORD says: "To the eunuchs who keep my Sabbaths, who choose what pleases me and hold fast to my covenant—to them I will give within my temple and its walls a memorial and a name better than sons and daughters; I will give them an everlasting name that will not be cut off.

This certainly indicates that there has been a change from the ceremonial law of Deuteronomy to the teaching found in Isaiah—but what could have occasioned such a change? The answer seems to be the earlier threat of the Canaanite religion. One of the earlier practices found in the Canaanite religion was the practice of male castration in connection with its worship practices. Therefore, for Israel to avoid any attempts to imitate Canaanite religious practice, there was a strong prohibition to one of its key features. But it appears that with the passage of time, the earlier prohibition was revised. The One who gave the Law, our Lord, had the freedom to revise it when the threat of a competing culture, such as that found in Moses' day, was lifted.

Likewise, in the ceremonial law that prohibited a Moabite or an Ammonite from the congregation of the Lord until the tenth generation (Deut. 23:3), there is the case of Ruth the Moabite, who not only entered the congregation of the Lord but also became an ancestor of David and of Jesus! Once again, the higher law of love transcended the straightforward Law even in the Old Testament.

The Law as God's Guidance for Holiness[6]

In the heart of the book of Romans, Paul's most systematic teaching on the doctrine of salvation, he placed his most sustained teaching on the proper use of the Law: Romans 9:30–10:13. Unfortunately, this text has also become the battleground over the pivotal text, "Christ is the end [or, as some translate it, "the goal"] of the Law" (Rom. 10:4). One group says that Christ's first coming

---

6. Walter C. Kaiser, Jr., "The Law as God's Gracious Guidance for the Promotion of Holiness" in *Five Views on Law and Gospel, ed.* Stanley N. Gundry Grand Rapids: Zondervan, 1999), 177–200; idem, "The Weightier and Lighter Matters of the Law: Moses, Jesus and Paul" in *Current Issues in Biblical and Pauline Interpretation: Studies in Honor of Merrill C. Tenney Presented by His Former Students,* ed. Gerald F. Hawthorne (Grand Rapids: Eerdmans, 1975), 176–192.

marked the "termination" for the Law's usefulness to us, and the other group says that Christ was the "goal" (or, the goal posts) towards which the whole Law was heading. It is this latter view that we are advocating here.

Paul began this section in Romans 9:30 with his repeated phrase that showed this was the next step in his argument, "What then shall we say?" The problem Paul tackles here was this: How did it happen that the Gentiles attained "righteousness by faith," while the Jewish people failed to attain the same righteousness, even though they pursued it "by works"—"as if that were possible?" And it was not possible to attain it by works, of course!

Israel's failure to achieve the "righteousness of God" was traced by Paul to five specific indictments against his fellow Jews in Romans 9:30–10:13:

1. Rather than receiving this righteousness by faith, Israel "[made] a law [out] of righteousness" (Greek: *nomon dikaiasynes*—Rom. 9:31) in their oral law. (Note the *order* of the Greek terms.) The fact that Paul reversed the two terms, placing "Law" first and the "righteousness" speaks strongly to the point that they "made a law *out of* righteousness."

2. Israel pursued this righteousness "as if it were [possible] by works" (Greek, *ek ergon;* Rom. 9:32), but it wasn't possible.

3. While many Gentiles believed in Christ, many Jewish people refused to believe in Messiah; he became instead the "stone that causes men to stumble and a rock that makes them fall" (9:33; quoting Isa. 8:14; 28:16). So they tripped over [the stone] Jesus as the Messiah!

4. While it must be conceded that the Jewish people were zealous for God, "their zeal [was] not based on knowledge" (Rom. 10:2). It was a self-help type of righteousness!

5. Finally, in place of the righteousness that came from God, all too many Jewish people had decided "to establish their own righteousness" (Rom. 10:3) as a homemade variety of righteousness that was not God's type of righteousness at all.

In the context of Romans 9:30–10:13, two different ways of attaining righteousness are being sharply contrasted: the way of faith in the stone Jesus and the way of works. However, God's righteousness could never be attained by way of works in either testament—not even as a hypothetical possibility. Galatians 3:21 teaches that "For if a law had been given that could impart life, then righteousness would certainly have come by the law." But such a law was not possible—no even hypothetically.[7] Moreover, another indication that they were on the wrong track is seen in the fact that they refused to believe in the Messiah. Added to this fault was another among the nation of Israel: they had insisted on establishing their own self-made righteousness rather than the righteousness described by Moses in the Torah. Homemade righteousness is not the same as divinely taught righteousness. In fact, this was the divinely described righteousness that also came from Moses (Rom. 10:5). Moses taught the same in two separate texts: Leviticus 18:5 and Deuteronomy 30:12–14. Some want to contrast the first text:

> The man who does these things will live by them (or "live in the sphere of them")[8]

with the second text, quoted by Paul in Romans 10:5, wherein Moses also taught:

> Do not say in your heart, "Who will ascend into heaven?" [that is, to bring Christ down] or "Who will descend into the deep?" [that is, to bring Christ up from the dead]. But what does it say? "**The word is near you; it is in your mouth and in your heart**," that is, the word of faith we are proclaiming: That if you confess with your mouth, "Jesus is Lord," and believe in your heart that God raised him from the dead, you will be saved" (emphasis added).

The apostle Paul concluded this case for the law best of all. He wrote in 1 Timothy 1:8–10:

> We know that the law is good if one uses it properly. We also know that the law is made not for the righteous, but for lawbreakers and rebels, the ungodly and sinful, the unholy and irreligious, for those who kill their fathers and mothers, for murderers, for the sexually immoral, for those practicing homosexuality, for slave traders and liars and perjurers—and for whatever else is contrary to sound doctrine (NIV).

---

7. See Alva J. McClain, *Law and Grace* (Chicago: Moody, 1954), 17.
8. See J. Oliver Buswell, *A Theology of the Christian Religion* (Grand Rapids: Zondervan, 1963), 1:313 for this better rendering of Lev. 18:5; Rom. 10:5.

Here we see that the moral law of God does have an always contemporary application—it restrains, rebukes, and condemns ungodly and criminal behavior. Without a transcendent lawgiver, humanity is left with only subjective and relative morals and laws, which can be changed to suit the tenor of the times. In an age where the trajectory of many social movements is toward unlimited personal autonomy and freedom, the Law of God remains an objective, eternal witness to that which is good, righteous, and holy.

Conclusion

1. The moral law of God as found in the Decalogue and the holiness code of Leviticus 18–20 provide the absolute norms for our living today in the *principles* they set forth.

2. The ethics of the Old Testament are "God-centered" and not ethnically oriented or chronologically limited.

3. Old Testament Law begins in the environment of grace for God delivered Israel from slavery before he commanded them to obey.

4. The laws are theocentric in that they relate all of life in its fullness to God, the Giver of Life.

Discussion Questions

1. How do you reconcile Jesus' teaching on the law in Matthew 5:17–20 with Paul's teaching in Romans 7:4–6?

2. Is the Law one whole teaching or did Jesus distinguish between some parts of the Law that were "heavier," or of greater priority?

3. How can we say that the environment of the Law is God's grace? What does that mean for keeping the Law?

4. Does not the Law of Deuteronomy 23:1 on becoming an eunuch contradict Isaiah 56:3–5? How can this be explained? What about the Law

in Deuteronomy 23:3 and its implications for Ruth the Moabite being in the Messianic line of Christ?

5. How does Romans 9:30–10:30 show how God's law can become a guide for holiness today?

6

The God of Monogamy or the God of Polygamy?

Question: *Is the God of the Old Testament the God who ordained one man-one woman marriage or the God who approved of polygamy?*

Genesis 2:21–24 presents the first man and woman in a monogamous marriage, which from that time on was described in Scripture as the normative pattern for marriage or the will of God in such relationships. From the early days of creation until the time of the patriarchs in Genesis 12–50, the forefathers from Adam to Noah in the line of Seth, all followed the monogamous example of the first man and woman with one exception—Lamech. Polygamy—or more precisely, polygyny[1] appeared for the first time in the reprobate line of Cain for as we have noted, as Lamech became the first known polygamist when he married two women: Adah and Zilah (Gen. 4:19). Meanwhile, in the continuing line of the believing seed that stretched from Shem to Terah, the father of Abraham, there was not another recorded instance of polygamy. Nevertheless, polygamy continued to appear throughout the Old Testament, even though it was not divinely approved nor was it the kind of marriage that fulfilled God's purpose for the sexes.

---

1. *Polygamy* is a broader term meaning "to have more than one spouse." Two other terms are more precise: *Polygyny* refers to one man who has multiple wives while *polyandry* denotes one woman with multiple husbands. Since polygamy is the most commonly used term, it will be used here to refer to one man with multiple wives.

So what about polygamy? Was polygamy ever lawful in the Old Testament under any of the laws given by Moses or any of the other writers of Scripture? If the law governing marriage looked back to Genesis 2:24 as to what was normative and what was the divine standard for marriage, how did the practice of polygamy come into the Old Testament? Under whose authority did it appear, and did God in any sense approve of it? Is there any biblical evidence for even a temporary permission from God to override the general law on marriage given to Adam and Eve for any specialized reason?

The answer to these questions is clear: God never approved or allowed for his concept of marriage to allow for multiple wives. It might even be asked: "How far off is the legalization of polygamy in the states?" which seems to be a natural corollary of recent liberalization of sexual mores and ethics in America. If the Bible does not approve of multiple partners, where then can those who claim to have a Christian view find a biblical basis to approve and support this concept?

As defined by those governments, which recognize polygamy as a legitimate form of marriage today, polygamy is defined as a legally recognized marriage contract wherein a man may have more than one wife at the same time. The largest group in the world that still permits polygamy is the Islamic faith (although see below). Sometimes poorer countries argue its economic benefits as more children are born to help with production on family farms.

However, polygamy is still a major problem for the Christian church in the twenty-first century. It is a problem because of the teaching of Scripture and because of the large number of Christian converts who have come from a polygamous background, especially for the burgeoning number of Christian converts in Africa. Here the church has continued to show tremendous growth since 1900, especially among those who were practicing polygamy. The geographical center of Christianity—the worldwide demographic map that shows the distribution of Christian believers—is now located in the heart of the African continent. The growth of Christianity in Africa in the twentieth century is almost without precedent anywhere else on the globe.

Problems Related to Polygamy in the Old Testament

Two examples from the Old Testament Scriptures will help us to focus on the problems that commonly take place in polygamous families. The first comes from the family of Jacob in Genesis 29:8–30:10. Jacob had fled from his home due to the family turmoil following his theft of the firstborn birthright from older brother,

Esau. Arriving at his mother's homestead, he lived and worked with his uncle Laban in Upper Mesopotamia. Here he fell in love with Laban's daughter Rachel. After promising to work seven years in return for her hand in marriage, Laban tricked him on his wedding night, so that Jacob woke up with Rachel's sister, Leah, as his new bride instead of the expected Rachel. When he complained to Laban about such a rotten trick, he was told it was not proper in that part of the world to let the younger Rachel marry ahead of the older Leah. So in a new agreement worked out with Laban, Jacob resigned himself to work another seven years to marry Rachel in addition to his already consummated marriage with her sister Leah.

The resulting jealousy and competition that arose between Leah and Rachel, now Jacob's two wives, is a testimony that can be repeated from those who have lived in polygamous homes. The divine wisdom in having only one wife is seen in God's making Eve the sole wife for Adam, for no man is capable of loving two wives *equally* at the same time. He will always favor one wife over the other. This became all the more evident when two servant girls were also given to Jacob as wives (Bilhah and Zilpah), and raised the competition a notch higher when they bore children for Jacob.

Even the Qur'an, which governs the Islamic practice of polygamy, recognizes the tension posed by having more than one wife. Sura 4:129 says:

> You will never be able to do perfect justice between wives even
> if it is your ardent desire, so do not incline too much to one of
> them (by giving her more of your time and provision) so as to
> leave the other hanging (i.e., neither divorced nor married).[2]

Leah's experience was further confirmation of this truth, for despite her attempt to win Jacob's affection by bearing one child after another for him (Gen. 29:32, 34), Jacob continued to love barren Rachel more than Leah (Gen. 29:20, 30). It is hard, if not impossible, for a woman to share the affection and love of her husband with another woman. It is also true that another reason often given for engaging in polygamy is childlessness of a wife. Rachel, unable to bear children, presented children to Jacob at first through her servant girl Bilhah (Gen. 30:3).

---

2. *The Noble Quran: Interpretation of the Meanings of the Noble Qur'an in the English Language.* Muhammad Taqi-ud-Din Al-Hilali and Muhammad Muhsin Khan, trans. (Houston: Dar-us-Salam Publications, 1999).l

A second biblical example can be seen in the polygamous family from which the prophet Samuel came (1 Sam. 1:1–20). In this situation, the two wives of Elkanah (Hannah and Peninnah) caused emotional distress for each other due to the fact that Elkanah's wife, Hannah, was childless while Peninnah continued to be extremely fertile. Not until Hannah was later enabled by the Lord to conceive was the tension somewhat lessened in that household.

Is Polygamy a Form of Adultery?

What shall we say then? Is polygamy a form of adultery? Can a practicing polygamous family be true and consistently obedient believers in Christ? Are there in some situations such overriding cultural reasons or justifications for polygamy, at least in some societies, that would cause us to revise the teaching of Scripture? Do those factors seriously outweigh biblical warnings? Furthermore, how should a church handle new converts who come from a background of traditional polygamy where family patterns are already set? Must new believers immediately set free the wives that they married after the first wife and thereby force these released wives to fend for themselves in a society that often offers little or no place for respectable employment for women? Would that not lead to even more disastrous effects, such as a life of immorality (i.e., prostitution) for the wives who now are without a home, support, and a husband, as would be the case in many societies in the world today? Can husbands who come to Christ, already possessing a plural number of wives, be baptized, partake of communion, or be permitted to be an elder in the church or even be a pastor of a congregation, while still being a practicing polygamous husband?

Practical Reasons for Polygamy in Many Cultures

Though the following discussion of practical reasons cannot be construed as a biblical authorization of polygamy, it can help us gain a clearer picture of the problems and the issues that are involved for those in the Old Testament, in agricultural subsistence societies, and in cultures and societies today.

In order to maintain family continuity, the Old Testament did recognize the practice of Levirate marriage (from the Latin *levir*, "a husband's brother"), which might be construed of as a limited form of polygamy.

The institution known as Levirate Marriage (called *Yibum* in Hebrew) requires that a man marry the childless widow of his brother to produce a child who will carry the deceased brother's name, so that the deceased brother's name will not be forgotten. Levirate marriage is detailed in the book of Deuteronomy (25:5 ff.): "If brothers dwell together, and one of them shall die and have no child, the widow shall not be married to another man who is not his [her husband's] kin. Her husband's brother shall come unto her [have intercourse with her], and take her to him as a wife, and perform the duty of a husband's brother unto her. And it shall be that the firstborn that she bears shall carry the name of the brother that died so that his name not be blotted out of Israel."[3]

This practice was an obligation in the Law of Moses, and the arrangement provided for full marital relations for each wife in the marriage (Exod. 21:10). While some could argue that this is a biblically approved type of polygamy, it is not treated as the norm, but rather the exception. Furthermore, while it was seen an obligation to maintain a family's name (and thus standing in the community), a brother could refuse to fulfill his obligations to his deceased brother. In such a case, the *halitza* ceremony took place:

If the brother of the deceased refuses to marry the widow Deuteronomy explains that the wife then must go to the gate of the city where the Elders sit, and inform them that her brother-in-law has refused to marry her. The Elders then must call the brother to them, and if he states, "I will not marry her," the ceremony of the Removed Sandal (*halitza*) takes place. In this ceremony the widow loosens or removes the brother-in-law's shoe, spits in front of his face, and says, "So shall be done to a man who refuses to build up his brother's house." Only after this symbolic act is the widow free to marry who she likes.[4]

3. "Issues in Jewish Ethics: Levirate Marriage and *Halitza*," Jewish Virtual Library, http://www.jewishvirtuallibrary.org/jsource/Judaism/Halitza.html (accessed March 5, 2015).
4. Ibid.

In the New Testament, we see clear evidence that polygamy was never intended to be an accepted practice when Jesus forbids the possibility of men using the Mosaic law to carry out "serial polygamy." Some biblical scholars are in error to insist that Moses approved of the act of divorcing a spouse in Deuteronomy 24:1–3. Jesus clearly condemned such thinking in Matthew 19:4–6. Instead of reading the Deuteronomy text as an example of Moses merely permitting or accepting divorce when the husband were determined to opt out of the marriage, Jesus instead rightly insisted that men who divorced their wives must put that decision in writing so the wife (and community) knew where she stood. Otherwise he could verbally divorce her one day in order to play around that night with another woman and then declare the marriage was on again the next day. If the divorce was only verbally declared between the two of them, only he and the wife knew what had transpired in his oral declaration as he announced, "I divorce you, I divorce you, I divorce you" to her. Since no one else heard, who would be the wiser?

Furthermore, Moses also prohibited the man from returning to the divorced partner after he had married another. This prohibition demonstrates that God did not approve of polygamy, and that a man could not use divorce as a means to use a "back door" into polygamy. It also shows that Moses had the same prohibition against divorce as Jesus did!

Whereas in most polygamous societies having more than one wife was a matter of pride and a symbol of the obvious wealth for the man to be able to support more than one wife, for Jesus the real norm was for one woman and one man to form a permanent and legitimate marriage.

Some groups of nominal Christians or fringe sects maintain that there is a religious reason for polygamy, holding that a large number of children brings with it the eternal blessing from God. Psalm 127:3–5 is often cited as a biblical support for this view. This passage does argue for large families, but there is no trace of an accompanying argument for polygamy in the same context as the means to reach this objective.

Historically and even in the present day, polygamy is most frequently practiced in rural and traditional societies. It is used in these cultures to ensure the continuation and growth of the family, for uppermost in the minds of most in these settings is the need for children be added to the family to carry out necessary tasks in subsistence agriculture. Every marriage carries with it an implied expectation that children will result from this union of the man and woman. These children, especially male children, will be the means for carrying on and extending the prosperity of the family, clan, and tribe in poorer cultures. They also are the means of providing for the support and care of the parents in their old age as well. In the meantime, the children provide enough workers in the fields, which is the best way to expand the family's productivity.

This is why the birth of a male son is especially significant. Therefore, if one wife or if two wives are producing only female children, it is necessary, it was thought, to marry another woman who may produce a male child. In the event of sickness, or the sudden loss of children through sickness or accident, the goal is to have spare males available to take up the slack in field work.

If the husband's livelihood called for him to move nomadically from one location to another with his flocks or herds, different wives were needed at different locations during these seasonal migrations to cook for him and to be a sexual partner in the new location.

In families where females were born, some cultures allowed for the possibility of the family receiving a much–needed dowry for the marriage of the daughter as further support for the family. In most undeveloped cultures, an unmarried adult woman is both unacceptable and a further economic liability, since a woman usually had no other means of support.

Finally, if war broke out between clans and tribes, it would be necessary, so it was argued in the traditional cultures of Africa, for a large number of males to be available in case some were lost in the fighting.

At this point no mention has been made of the carnal desires of men, who often sought to have sex with more than one woman just for the thrill of doing so. One ancient example is King David, who was a victim of his own hormones as he committed adultery with Bathsheba (2 Sam. 11:26–27). Where these secret lustful desires are present, they needed to be recognized for what they were—sin!

Additional reasons are still being added in the present day for having polygamous marriages—with even less necessity, however, than that presented in traditional cultures. Some argue that if a first wife were to die in childbirth, by disease, or by accident the second wife could provide unbroken continuity and support that the family needed. Or, if the first wife was taken seriously ill, a second spouse was there to carry out family duties.

It is recognized that in some cultures, the first wife was sometimes allowed to have a voice in selecting the second wife. In other settings, the first wife would request that the husband marry another to help bear the workload of the family. A first wife may even suggest that a second wife be secured to provide for the husband's sexual needs during periods of culturally mandated abstinence (e.g., during extended times of nursing a child, which could last for two or three years).

The Biblical Treatment of Polygamy

The Bible never gave authorization or permission for polygamy. In addition to the first polygamist Lamech in Genesis 4, there is only one other passage prior to Noah's flood that provides a possible example of polygamy—Genesis 6:1–7. While there are various views about the identity of the "sons of God" in this passage, it is clear that their perversion involved some form of polygamy: "they took as their wives any they chose" (ESV). Regardless of who the "sons of God" were, one thing is clear about mankind at this point in history: "every intention of the thoughts of his heart was only evil continually." Such wickedness brought to pass the judgment of the Flood, killing all mankind. Such a response can hardly be interpreted as divine approval for polygamy.

Even during the two and a half centuries of the Patriarchal period (c. 2000–1750 BC) in Genesis 12–50, only four other examples of polygamy can be cited from Scripture:

1. Abraham's brother Nahor had a concubine.

2. Abraham was talked into having temporary sexual relations with Hagar, Sarah's handmaiden.

3. Esau, a profane person acting out of spite and reacting against the faith of his parents, took three wives.

4. Jacob married two sisters and received their handmaids as well.

Thus there were only six recorded examples of polygamy from the patriarchs until sometime around 1750 BC.

In the next period, there are thirteen examples, but twelve of these are about persons who possessed absolute power, usually as leaders of the people, and who autocratically made up their own rules as they went along. They included: in the book of Judges: Gideon, Jair, Ibzan, Abdon, Samson, one non-leader, Elhanah, Hannah's husband; and various kings: Saul, David, Solomon, Rehoboam, Abijah, Ahab, and Jehoram.[5]

---

5. These statistics are from S. E. Dwight, *The Hebrew Wife* (New York: Leavitt, 1836), 24–29.

The fact that seven of the thirteen were kings and five of the thirteen were judges (popularly recognized leaders prior to the monarch) would explain why no e*arthly* tribunal punished them or called them to accounts. Moreover, Scripture does not always pause to pass a moral comment on what it has just described. Yet it must be noticed that much of the misfortune that came on these men was rooted in the chaos of their domestic lives. For example, as a result of David's sin with Bathsheba, the biblical text specifically noted the effects this had on every person on the distaff side of the Davidic line of kings from that point forward until the Babylonian exile!

Scripture clearly demonstrates monogamous expectations in a number of texts. For example, the Ten Commandments states: "You shall not covet your neighbor's wife" (Exod. 20:17b). It does not say "your neighbor's wives." In discussing the judgment that will fall on the people if they forsake the covenant, Moses states that a man will be so desperate that he will not give food to "the wife he loves" (Deut. 28:54). He does not say "the wives he loves." Likewise, the Old Testament consistently refers to only to a single wife: "your wife as a fruit-ful vine" (Ps. 128:3); "rejoice in the wife of your youth" (Prov. 5:18); and "both the husband and the wife" (Jer. 6:11). The reference to one's "wife," rather than "wives," is routine in Scripture.

Those who do attempt to make a case for polygamy as permissible in the Bible usually point to four key biblical passages: Exodus 21:7–11; Leviticus 18:18; Deuteronomy 21:15–17; and 2 Samuel 12:7–8. These must be examined in order.

Exodus 21:7–11

> [7]If a man sells his daughter as a servant, she is not to go free as menservants do. [8]If she does not please the master who has se-lected her for himself, he must let her be redeemed. He has no right to sell her to foreigners, because he has broken faith with her. [9]If he selects her for his son, he must grant her the rights of a daughter. [10]If he marries another woman, he must not de-prive the first one of her food, clothing and marital rights. [11]If he does not provide her with these three things, she is to go free, without any payment of money.

There are three mistakes usually made in the modern translations of this text. The first is in verse 8, where the translators follow the Greek Septuagint rather than the Hebrew text by substituting the word "not" (Hebrew *lo'*) instead of retaining the words "for himself" (Hebrew *lo*). This preferred reading of "for himself" is also the accepted reading of all manuscripts and editions of the Samaritan Pentateuch, as well as the Syriac, Persian, and Arabic versions. The point then is that if the master does not betroth the girl, either to himself or to his son, he must let her be redeemed. But it does not permit or authorize a polygamous situation.

The second error is in verse 10, which incorrectly reads: "if he married another as wife." But verse 8 notes that the other woman had already been rejected; therefore it should read: "if he marries another woman instead of her." It is not that he is taking another wife *in addition* to this girl, but that he took another instead, or *in place of*, this girl.

The third mistake is also in verse 10. The word translated as "marital rights" is an improper guess at a word that is a *hapax legomenon,* that is, a word only occurring once in the Bible. That means we usually do not have enough contexts to show us how the word was used or what it meant. But since the same list of three items appears in Sumerian and Akkadian texts from the Ancient Near East and clearly mean "food, clothing, and *oil/ointments*." The translators have been misled by following the Septuagint (the Greek translation of the Old Testament), which translated the word as "her cohabitation." Therefore, "marital rights" is definitely a wrong translation.

Leviticus 18:18

Do not take your wife's sister as a rival wife and have sexual relations with her while your wife is living.

Two major interpretations have been suggested for this text: 1) Do not marry your wife's sister during the lifetime of your wife, for that would vex her while your wife is still living; or 2) Do not marry your sister-in-law, although you may marry one who is not her sister or even her sister after your first wife's death, because that will not vex her. On this second view, polygamy would be permitted as well as marriage to one's sister–in–law and sister of a deceased wife.

The problem is with the Hebrew phrase *a woman to her sister*, translated as "Do not take your wife's sister." While this phrase ordinarily means "one to another," polygamy is expressly forbidden by the institution of marriage in Genesis 2:24. Moreover, the incest prohibitions in Leviticus 18 forbid marriage between a woman and her brother-in-law, a nephew and an aunt, a mother and a son, an uncle and a niece, a father and a daughter. The prohibitions in Leviticus are based on the closeness of the relationship. Such would be the case in a marriage between a man and his sister-in-law. Therefore, this text is a single prohibition against polygamy in keeping with the law against incest.

Deuteronomy 21:15–17

[15]If a man has two wives, and he loves one but not the other, and both bear him sons but the firstborn is the son of the wife he does not love, [16]When he wills his property to his sons, he must not give the rights of the firstborn to the sons of the wife he loves in preference to his actual firstborn, the son of the wife he does not love. [17]He must acknowledge the son of his unloved wife as the firstborn by giving him a double share of all that he has. That son is the first sign of his father's strength. The right of the firstborn belongs to him.

From this law, some form the following syllogism and argue for the legitimacy of polygamy. It goes this way:

MAJOR PREMISE: Moses is legislating on the case of a man who has two wives at the same time.

MINOR PREMISE: But Moses could not lawfully legislate on that which might not lawfully exist.

CONCLUSION: To have two wives at the same time was therefore lawful.

S. E. Dwight's rejoinder was to attack the minor premise.[6] He quoted Deuteronomy 23:18, which legislated on the wages for a harlot, but which practice Moses immediately condemned as being "an abomination to the Lord," and stating, "There shall be no harlot of the daughters of Israel." Thus, legislation on a practice in no way authorized that practice, as this argument wants to contend.

---

6. Dwight, *The Hebrew Wife*, 20.

The assumption that this text sanctions polygamy is based on a careless reading of Deuteronomy 21:15. As shown by the subsequent verbs in this text, the text should read, "If a man has had two wives." But one of those wives has already passed away, and a second has been chosen. Therefore, the teaching of the text is that the first wife, who was hated, has now died, and he has subsequently married another wife. The birthright cannot be taken away from the first wife's eldest son and given to the firstborn of the new wife on the death of the first wife.

2 Samuel 12:7b–8

7b This is what the LORD, the God of Israel says: "I anointed you king over Israel, and I delivered you from the hand of Saul. 8I gave your master's house to you, and your master's wives in your arms."

This reading appears at a first glance to give divine approval for polygamy, but such a conclusion is the result of a superficial reading of the text. The fact is that Saul's wives did not become part of David's wives or his harem. The only two wives Saul had were Ahinoam, the daughter of Ahimaaz (1 Sam. 14:50) and mother of Michal, David's wife; and Rizpah (2 Sam. 3:7). Moreover, the biblical penalty for marrying one's mother-in-law was to be burnt alive (Lev. 20:14), so David surely did not commit this crime!

David's wives are enumerated several times: 2 Samuel 2:2 and 3:2–5; 1 Chronicles 3:1–9. Even after Saul's death, Saul's wives are never listed as part of David's wives. David did have a wife by the name of Ahinoam, but she is to be distinguished from a woman by the same name known as Saul's wife for this Ahinoam was from Jezreel. Additionally, David had married her during Saul's lifetime.

So what about 2 Samuel 12:8? A comma should be placed after the word *house,* and the word translated as "wives" should be translated "women." Both the "house" and the "women," therefore, were given to David as a "possession," not into his "bosom" or "arms" as some versions have so infelicitously translated the term. It is better to render the Hebrew word as the NASB renders it, into David's "care."

Polygamy never was God's order of things for marriage even though it appeared in biblical times. The best teaching on monogamous marriages is Proverbs 5:15–21. Polygamy, on the other hand, is an act of rebellion against the will of God, for first of all it breaks a solemn marriage vow made to God who is a party to the marriage covenant (Prov. 2:17; Mal. 2:13–15). Then the vow was made with his spouse, and the vow was made to God before witnesses. As such, polygamy is also a betrayal of the wife he originally married and needs to be handled as a case of adultery in church discipline.

Should Polygamists Be Permitted to be Pastors or Elders in the Church?

On this point, the Bible is also clear: An elder must be the husband of one wife (1 Tim. 3:1–2). God wanted a godly model of monogamy to be the pattern set before his people and modeled by his elders and pastors.

In areas of the world where a polygamous man has been converted and, after some time of walking with the Lord, decides he is being called to serve the Lord as an elder or pastor, the issue of his polygamy must be dealt with. As a result of prayer, counseling, and the teaching of the word of God, an agreed upon method for handling the setting aside of a second wife or multiple wives and providing for lifetime support must be worked out before he can assume a position of leadership.

Conclusion

It is all too common today to see statements by Christian theologians or Christian anthropologists and sociologists to the effect that any prohibition of polygamy on Scriptural grounds is on very shaky grounds. Thus, Karl Barth, for example, intoned: "We can hardly point with certainty to a single text in which polygamy is expressly forbidden and monogamy is universally decreed. If, then, we approach the Bible legalistically, we cannot honestly conclude that in this matter we are dealing with an unconditional law of God."[7] Likewise, Oswald Fountain disappointingly found that the church's case against polygamy was "on the basis of Scripture a flimsy one."[8] But notice such complaints usually come

---

7. Karl Barth, *Church Dogmatics* (Edinburg: T & T Clark, 1957), 3–4:199.
8. Oswald C. Fountain, "Polygamy and the Church," in *Missiology: An International Review,* 11 1974), 111. Other contributors to this topic are: E. G. Parrinder, *The Bible and Polygamy,* (London: SPCK, 1958); Willard Bruce, "Polygamy and the Church," in *Concordia Theological Monthly,* 34 (1963): 223–32; Robert Holst, "Polygamy and the Bible," in *International Review of Missions,* 56 (1967): 205–13; Eugene Hillman, "Polygamy Reconsidered," in *Practical Anthropology,* 17 (1970): 60–74; Nathaniel G. N. Inyamah, "Polygamy and the Christian Church," in *Concordia Theological Monthly* 43 (1972): 138–43; Thomas S. Piper, "Did God Condone Polygamy?" *Good News Broadcaster* 35 (1977): 28.

with a number of qualifying words such as Barth's "hardly," "with certainty," "expressly," and "universally." It is as if God merely suggested monogamy, but he never enforced it as the normative view and practice. In Leviticus 18:18, in the midst of the laws of regarding affinity, the Word of God teaches: "Neither shall you take one wife to another in her lifetime to vex her."

In like manner, there are five New Testament texts that built on the original teaching in Genesis 2:24. They are Matthew 5:31–32; 19:3–9; Mark 10:2–12; Luke 16:18; and 1 Corinthians 7:1–2, which says, "each man is to have his own wife, and each woman her own husband." In light of such clear teaching, it is wrong for Christian teachers to dismiss out of hand such texts and to suggest that perhaps monogamy was not the divinely authorized way for marriages. God has ordained that *one man* and *one woman* should come together to form a marriage.

Discussion Questions

1. How do you understand the divine command in Genesis 2:24–26 in light of the thirteen examples of polygamy in the early chapters of the Bible?

2. What are some of the practical problems of polygamy or polyandry (several husbands for one wife)?

3. What translation mistakes do the English versions make in rendering the Hebrew text of Exodus 21:7–11?

4. Did God give Saul's wives to King David in 2 Samuel 12:7b–8? What evidence can you give to the contrary?

5. How should the Christian church respond to converts who already are polygamists and who wish to answer the call of God to the ministry or to be an elder or deacon in the church?

6. How is Proverbs 5:15–23 a powerful teaching on monogamy?

7

The God Who Rules Satan or the God Who Battles Satan?

Question: *Is the God of the Old Testament the God who rules over Satan and all evil or is he a God who must battle against Satan to overcome him?*

Of all the major personalities in the Bible, Satan is perhaps the most enigmatic. Christians assume that after Genesis 3, everything that is bad or evil is the work of Satan. Yet it can legitimately be asked, Is Satan even mentioned in the Old Testament, much less responsible for all the evil that is attributed to him? In reality, his name appears so seldom that one wonders if the writers of the older testament were really aware of his existence or his work. It almost seems that we have to wait until the New Testament times before his persona and activities became a matter of concern. Or is that a misrepresentation of the real situation?

The Old Testament begins with God creating everything and everyone in the cosmos, thus even evil cannot be excluded from the purview of God's permissive work in the world. But to affirm this statement raises an interesting problem: Why then did he create Satan and his angels? Were they always as they are now? For what purpose did God create them? What do we know about this leader of evil, his minions, and how he became the source of so much trouble on earth, especially from reading the Old Testament alone? Was it simply because of God's love of freedom in his creatures that he allowed such an evil supernatural force to foment all of this wickedness, if we are to attribute it all evil to him? There is more to ponder here than we normally can stretch our minds around, much less respond with solid answers. So, what are we to make of Satan's presence and the reality of evil in the Old Testament? The whole Christian message was to deal with the presence of sin in our world, so believers take evil as being real. Neither are believers in doubt as to how good and evil will eventually end up, for when Christ died, the gauntlet was thrown down in the resurrection of Jesus Christ. Good will win. Our problem, however, is why did God ever allow evil in the first place? What is the origin of evil?

The Risks of Emphasizing the Demonic

There is a danger, of course, in overemphasizing the demonic and the topic of evil spirits, wickedness, Satan, and the netherworld. Israel was given clear warnings in Leviticus 20:6 and Isaiah 8:19 not to engage in the use of magic or to consult wizards that "peep and mutter." In fact, Deuteronomy 18:9–13 warned that when Israel entered the land of Canaan, they were not to imitate the detestable ways of the nations in that place. They were warned against: sacrificing their sons and daughters in the fire; practicing divination or sorcery; interpreting omens; engaging in witchcraft; casting spells; or consulting mediums, spiritists, or inquiring for information from the dead. The reason all these forms and practices were prohibited was because God had sent his Word to Israel through his prophets, particularly through that final prophet who was to come, the Messiah (Deut. 18:14–22). Therefore, there was no need to get any "inside" information from sources in the netherworld; God had spoken clearly enough!

But there was also a practical reason for this prohibition from a theological point of view: involvement with the demonic presented the possibility of developing a dualism or polytheism, much like that of the societies that surrounded them. The first commandment strictly announced: "You shall have no other gods before me" (Exod. 20:3; cf. Deut. 29:16–17; Isa. 44:9–20).

It bears special notice that God was so intent that He be worshipped exclusively that there are only three Old Testament passages where "Satan" is specifically mentioned: Job 1–2; Zechariah 3:1–2; and 1 Chronicles 21:1. Thus, Israel's focus was instead to be on the Lord and not on the sponsor of evil and wickedness. Biblical revelation stressed that one should have trust in the Lord rather than concentrating on all the possible evil that was in the world.

A Heavenly Assembly

One of the most curious passages in the Bible is found in Deuteronomy 32:8–9. The rendering in the Revised Standard Version states:

> When the Most High gave to the nations their inheritance,
> when he separated the sons of men,
> he fixed the bounds of the people according to the number
> of the sons of God.
> For the LORD's [Yahweh's] portion is his people,
> Jacob his allotted heritage.

In this poetic passage, the text suggests that Israel (also here called "Jacob") belonged to Yahweh as his heritage while the people of the other nations belonged to the "sons of God." This reading must have seemed offensive to the Rabbis, so they read it later to say that the peoples of the nations belonged to the "sons of Israel," which made this text even more enigmatic to interpret. The Septuagint, a third century BC Greek translation of the Old Testament, rendered this phrase "angels of God," instead of the Jewish rendering of "sons of Israel." However, when a portion of the Dead Sea Scrolls containing this passage came to light, it too read "sons of God," thereby vindicating the RSV reading of the text.

This seemed to match the presence of the "gods" or the "sons of the Most High" in Psalm 82. In that psalm, "God presides over the great assembly; he gives judgment among the 'gods'" (Ps. 82:1). This psalm is unique among those in the Psalter for it portrays God as presiding over the divine assembly, but yet rebuking the sons of the gods for their dereliction of their duties. This brief allusion seems to argue for the real existence of a heavenly court or assembly where God himself holds divine council and accuses the "gods" for failing to exercise their duties of protecting those who are poor and powerless. Could it be that Satan himself showed up at such a council meeting, as described in the book of Job (1–2)? Were some or all of these fallen angels or demons?

Job is described as a man who was "blameless and upright," one who "feared God" (Job 1:1). But then, "One day the angels came to present themselves before the LORD, and Satan also came with them" (Job 1:6). Satan had previously been "roaming through the earth, going back and forth in it" (1:7) when he too made his appearance at the heavenly court.

But to return to Psalm 82, God roundly condemned the "sons of the gods" for failing to administer justice, for they had showed partiality in favor of the wicked, while the fatherless, the weak, the afflicted, and the destitute received no help or justice from these "sons." As a result, the Psalm (82:8) calls on God to arise and to take over the task of judging the earth, for all the nations are the inheritance of the Lord.

But who were these "sons of gods/God"? They appear to be superhuman beings, but some argue that they refer only to mere human beings. It is true that human "judges" are referred to as "Elohim" (a word normally rendered elsewhere as "God") in the NIV translation of Exodus 21:6 and 22:8–9, but other translations such as the RSV, NEB, JB, or NRSV do not use that rendering of "judges" here. In fact, the translation of "Elohim" for "judges" could also appear in Psalms 58:11; 138:1 and Exodus 22:28, but it does not appear in any of the translations either at these places.

Psalm 82:7 ("but you will die like mere men") says that the sons of God/gods will die like men, so they may not be immortal or supernatural beings. But they must still be understood to be some type of celestial beings, which is the prevailing interpretation of this psalm. They were all denizens of heaven who were created by and subordinate to Yahweh and who were expected to do the work God gave them to do.

Nevertheless, there is a strong argument against this supernatural understanding that is attributed to Jesus. In John 10:34–36, in a dispute with the Jews over Jesus' claim to be God, Jesus cites verse 34, "I have said you are gods" (Psalm 82:6), which appears to argue conclusively that "sons of God" cannot be equated with supernatural beings in Psalm 82. But that is not as straightforward and simple a matter as it seems, for Jesus does not explicitly endorse a either interpretation of Psalm 82. Jesus seems to be using an *a fortiori* argument[1] in John 10:34–36, where a comparison between one who is in the nature of God and angels, who are called "gods," is said to be just as relevant as a comparison between God and humans; thus the contrast is still between the Creator himself and his created beings. Even so, one still must be careful to note that the functions given to the "sons of God/gods" with regard to the poor, the weak and the destitute are jobs clearly given to humans elsewhere in Scripture.

---

1. An *a fortiori* argument draws upon a stronger, conclusive statement to support a weaker or less conclusive statement. In common usage it is used to mean "even more certain," or "all the more so."

A more direct reference to such a heavenly court comes from the account of the despised prophet Micaiah and his contest with the false prophets in 1 Kings 22 and 2 Chronicles 18. Jehoshaphat, the king of Judah, was asked to join King Ahab, king of Israel, to recover the city of Ramoth Gilead. As was discussed in chapter five, King Jehoshaphat impulsively agreed to help, but then inquired if there was a prophet of Yahweh who would validate the counsel of four hundred false prophets, from whom Ahab had just received assurances that this Israelite-Judean alliance would be successful. It turned out that Ahab had one such Yahweh prophet in prison, Micaiah, a true servant of God.

When Micaiah was summoned, he was told about a vision that had been given that involved a meeting of a divine council where Yahweh asked who would go and entice King Ahab to attack Ramoth Gilead, during which the king would be killed in battle. One spirit came forth and offered to become a lying spirit in the mouth of Ahab's four hundred prophets. Yahweh agreed to this plan and urged that spirit to go and carry out that mission. Note that the setting for this vision is a meeting of the heavenly council, a scene similar to the prologue in Job 1–2.

Some have argued that this "lying spirit" is none other than Satan himself for in 1 Kings 22:21 this text uses the definite article, *haruah*, "the spirit." But the word Satan does not occur in this account, thus the article may simply be a generic definite article meaning "a spirit." The reason for making this spirit "evil" is because he performs an evil function: he prompts Ahab's prophet to speak lies and thus to deceive. Moreover, the text makes a distinction between the spirit that inspires Micaiah and the one who influences the 400 prophets of Ahab. One of Ahab's prophets asked sarcastically, "Which way did the spirit from the LORD go when he went from me to speak to you?" (1 Kings 22:24; 2 Chron. 18:23), thus Micaiah and Ahab's prophets could not have received their messages from the same source. In this instance, as in others in the Old Testament, one must distinguish between the decretive will of God and the permissive will of God. God permitted the author of evil to do his worse, but it still came out to the praise of God's glory.

The Serpent of Genesis 3

If many Christians are asked to identify the first biblical reference to Satan or the Devil in the Bible, they would point to Genesis 3. However, Satan's name does not appear there. Instead, we are told right from the first verse, "Now the serpent was more crafty than the wild animals the LORD God had made." It is

important to note that the word "serpent" always appears with the Hebrew article, *han-nahash*, and that the Hebrew preposition "from" can be rendered either
as a partitive form meaning "any of the wild animals," (which is how the same
expression in Genesis 3:1 is rendered in most English versions) or in a comparative sense meaning "more than" or "above all the wild animals" (which is how
Genesis 3:14 is rendered in most English versions). However, as noted above,
the Hebrew form is exactly the same in both Genesis 3:1 and Genesis 3:14.

It is best, however, to take it as a comparative form in both instances. This
means that "the serpent" is not treated as one of the animals, nor should he be,
because he has the ability to use human speech. It also reveals that he has pre-
ternatural knowledge of what God had said in the garden, and he furthermore
directly impugns God's motives when he says "You certainly will not die . . . for
God knows that when you eat, your eyes will be opened and you will be like
God" (3:4–5). Add to these reasons the fact that when "the serpent" is cursed, he
too is treated as a responsible moral agent and not as a brute beast. The fact that
the curse is also ongoing removes the identity of the serpent from any human
natural aversion to reptiles or snakes. The Serpent is no less than Satan himself
in this context!

What are the identities that are given to the Serpent by others? One suggestion is that he has the features of the "monsters" of ancient mythology. Some
point to forms of ancient myth related to Tiamat, the Mesopotamian dragon
goddess of chaos and darkness (also associated with serpents), to Yam, the sea
monster of chaos, or to Mot, the west Semitic god of death. Another view is
that he is associated with the serpents of the fertility religions of Canaan and
the ancient Near East. Still another suggestion is that the serpent represents a
demon, but which demonic influence has now been suppressed. But the most
ancient of the interpretations for "the serpent" is that he is the embodiment or
representation of Satan. This identification appears in the pre-Christian period
in the apocryphal book *Wisdom of Solomon* (usually dated to the first or second
century BC), where we read: "God created man for incorruption, and made him
in the image of his own eternity, but through the devil's envy, death entered the
world" (Wisd. 2:23–24, RSV).

The allusion to the temptation of Eve is apparent. Added to this list of suggestions is the more certain identification found in the New Testament. John
8:44 called Satan "a murderer from the beginning" and the "father of lies."
Even more dramatically, the apostle Paul spoke of God's crushing of Satan
under the feet of believers in Romans 16:20 (an obvious allusion to Genesis

3:15), while the apostle John in Revelation 12:5 and 20:2 identified Satan as "the ancient serpent."

Nevertheless, in spite of all this documentation, many modern scholars reject the identification of "the serpent" with Satan because they claim a developed doctrine of Satan is very late in the history of Judaism. To put forth such an identity would, in their view, be anachronistic and beyond the pale of the meaning of the author of Genesis 3; it would be reading a meaning from the New Testament back into the Old Testament.

But such a conclusion is a modern difficulty that was not shared by the early church that understood Genesis 3:15, at least, to be a prophecy that announced the future defeat of Satan by Messiah.[2] They called this text the *protoevangelium,* the "first gospel." Moreover, they viewed the reference to "he will crush your head" to be understood in a collective sense, where a sole representative of the group is signified as well as the whole group in what is known as corporate solidarity. The meaning then oscillated back and forth between the one "Seed," who was a representative of the many, and the "seed" as the whole group made up of all believers. This is can be seen in the third century BC translation of the Septuagint where the Greek text expresses grammatical agreement between the relative pronoun and antecedent in gender and number over 150 times in the book of Genesis; but in this one case in the whole book of Genesis, the translators broke their otherwise irrevocable rule. They left the relative masculine pronoun "he" (Greek, *autos*) not to agree with the neuter antecedent of "seed" (Greek, *sperma*), thus pointing to a male descendant of Eve as the victor over Satan. Clearly, even before the Messiah came as a babe in Bethlehem (by almost some three hundred years later than this translation), there was an expectancy of the Messiah who would win the contest with Satan.

The Satan of Job

The Hebrew word translated "Satan" means an "adversary," or "opponent" (Hebrew *satan)* Thus, one of Solomon's enemies was Rezon, who ruled in Aram/Syria; he was an "adversary" as long as Solomon lived (1 Kings 11:25, *satan*). But this word also means "accuser," or "prosecuting attorney" in contexts where legal proceedings are involved, e.g., Psalm 109:6 and its cognate verb in Psalms

---

2. Christian apologists Justin Martyr (*Dialogue with Trypho*) and Irenaeus (*Against Heresies*) made this identification in the second century AD.

109:4, 20, 29. The same word also appears in Job 1:6–9, 12 and 2:1–4 6–7, where it also appears with the definite article.

But how is the figure of "the Satan" regarded in Job? Some allege that Satan's role in that book is one of a prosecuting attorney who is divinely charged with the responsibility of exposing human sinfulness. In that case he might not be inherently evil, but could be a loyal servant of God.

In two scenes in Job 1:6–12 and 2:1–6, however, Satan presents himself, along with other supernatural beings, before Yahweh at the heavenly council or divine assembly. These scenes cannot be equated with the mythology of Israel's pagan neighbors for the members of this heavenly court in the Bible are all subordinate beings who are bounded by the will of Yahweh. In the pagan mythologies, the deities do as they please and show themselves to be willful as each challenges the other for supremacy. Whether Satan was a regular member of Yahweh's assembled entourage or not is not certain for the text seems to imply that he was not usually in attendance at the divine assembly.

When Yahweh inquired where Satan had come from, he responded by saying he had come from scouring the earth looking for human evidence of sinfulness and failings. Some interpreters assign the role of a prosecutor to him, noting that the Persian king had secret agents who monitored the loyalty of his subjects, but this evidence comes too late in time for the book of Job, which seems better located in patriarchal times (2000–1750 BC) rather than the Persian period in the sixth century BC.

Nevertheless, it was Yahweh who directed Satan's attention to Job as a person of outstanding integrity and piety (1:8). This thesis is not rejected by Satan, but he does impugn Job's motives (1:9–11) alleging that Job only "fears God" because God has set a protective hedge around Job that has made Job both prosperous and wealthy. Yahweh consents to Satan's proposed testing of Job in Job 1:12, but God lays down a condition: Satan is not allowed to touch Job's person, that is, to attack him physically.

The scene shifts back to earth in Job 1:13–22 as news of one calamity after another comes by messengers who had hardly finished telling their tale of woe when another messenger arrives with additional reports of grief (1:16–18). Even though Job is still unaware of Satan's role in all that is happening, Job instead points to the hand of God as his stay in all of this trouble (1:21).

In the second meeting of the divine assembly, Yahweh once more calls special attention to his servant Job (2:3), for 1:22 had recorded that "In all this, Job did not sin by charging God with wrongdoing." Satan suggests that Job will curse God if his health is attacked (2:4), but before the test can be resumed, once more God restricts Satan by saying Satan may attack Job's body, but his life must be spared (2:6). Satan proceeded to afflict Job's body from his head to his feet, but 2:7 is the last we hear of Satan's involvement in this case; he had been proven to be incorrect about the faithfulness of one of God's followers. Satan does not even appear in the epilogue of 42:7–17, nor does Yahweh refer to Satan when he directly confronts Job in Job 38–41.

Satan acted in Job just as 1 Peter 5:8 noted: he goes about "like a roaring lion looking for someone to devour." Satan not only assumed the role of accusing Christians before God in Job, but also in Revelation 12:10. And even though Satan desired to sift the apostle Peter like one sifts wheat, just as he had sifted Job, Jesus prayed for Peter that his faith would not fail (Luke 22:31).

Satan in Zechariah

In the fourth of the eight night visions given to the prophet Zechariah in 520 BC, the Lord showed Zechariah a depiction of Joshua, the high priest, dressed in filthy clothes "standing before the angel of the LORD, and [the] Satan [who again appears with the definite article indicating it is a title rather than a proper name] standing at his right side to accuse him" (3:1). As in the account of Job, Satan is once more depicted as being in the angelic company in his role as the accuser of the brethren. This may well be but another scene of the heavenly council, but of this we cannot be certain.

The high priest Joshua is described as wearing filthy clothes because he is bearing his own sin and the sin and guilt of his fellow Judeans. But in verse 4 the angel said to those who were standing in front of him, "Take off his filthy clothes," for his sin had been taken away and costly new garments were given to him.

The angel of the Lord instructed him, "This is what the LORD Almighty says: 'If you will walk in my ways and keep my requirements, then you will govern my house and have charge of my courts, and I will give you a place among those standing here" (3:7). The impurity, whether it came from their own sin or the contamination of the Babylonian exile from which they had recently returned, would both be taken away.

The reference to Satan in this text is brief, but he is represented as a prosecutor who brings charges against mortals before God. Therefore, his work and attitudes are not only inimical to human beings, they are also opposed to God as well. This last point can be affirmed by the rebuke of God in Zechariah 3:2, "The LORD said to Satan, 'The LORD rebuke you, Satan! The LORD who has chosen Jerusalem rebuke you!'" Satan is antagonistic to God's gracious dealings with his people, but he is also antagonistic to God as well.

Satan in 1 Chronicles

First Chronicles 21:1 begins to describe a narrative in which David ordered a census of the people of Israel even though his commander-in-chief of the army, Joab, strongly objected to such. "Satan rose up against Israel and incited David to take a census of Israel." Of special note is the fact that this is the first time that Satan appears without the definite article.

So displeased was God with this action that he determined to punish the nation for this action, and therefore offered David three different punishments to choose from (1 Chron. 21:11–12). From these David choose a three-day plague. God in his mercy, however, later commanded the plague to stop. It happened that at the time the angel, who was carrying out the punishment, was at the threshing floor of a Jebusite named Araunah. David purchased that property from Araunah, which later on became the site of Israel's temple site in Jerusalem.

Satan plays no further part in this account than his inciting David to number his troops. The calling for such a census involved what would be tantamount to a call-up of the troops; but this was an imperialistic move on David's part for God had not ordered him to go into battle nor was he to arbitrarily add territory to his domain unless directed by God to do so. So Satan was the inciter of this action, but it is not as if God were not sovereign. In 2 Samuel 24:1 it is said that Yahweh incited David to take this census. This is a perfect example of seeing what God permits can also be directly attributed to him. The writer of 1 Chronicles did not emend what God had said earlier to the writer of 2 Samuel; but Yahweh is sovereign over every detail and action that goes on in the earth so he must either direct it or permit it.

The Fall of Satan in Isaiah 14:12–15 and Ezekiel 28:12–19

In two funeral dirges that lamented the death of a pagan king, the king of Babylon and the king of Tyre, both of whom had exalted themselves beyond normal limits, descriptions can be found of the original fall of Satan from his once cherished position in the heavenly realms. These passages appear to be more like mock laments that are loaded with sarcasm and exaggerated metaphor.

Isaiah 14:12 begins a lament by saying, "How you have fallen from heaven, O morning star, son of the dawn! You have been cast down to the earth, you who once laid low the nations." These words are addressed to the king of Babylon, who then is quoted as boasting, "I will ascend to heaven; I will raise my throne above the stars of God; I will sit enthroned on the mount of assembly, on the utmost heights of the sacred mountain. I will ascend above the tops of the clouds; I will make myself like the Most High" (14:13–14). These obviously hyperbolic (exaggerated) expressions cause us to look beyond the immediate historical references to other events that could be identified with this description.

This is similar to the interpretive method of the ancient church of Antioch in the fourth and fifth centuries A.D. Their interpretive view is called *theoria*, based the Greek word meaning "to look at, consider, or speculate."[3] The Antiochian view rejected any and all double or dual meanings of Scripture (in opposition to the Alexandrian School in Egypt of Origen) and instead strenuously argued for a view that saw the near-historical reference to share, at one and the same time, its immediate meaning with a distant, future, or remote happening, with which there were parallel descriptions. The clue to its presence in the text was its use of hyperbolic language that exceeded the historical reference.

A simple example of this would be when an Olympic marksman looks down the sights of a rifle. He (or she) aligns the rear site with the front sight and then aligns both with the ultimate distant target. To hit the bull's-eye, all three elements must be in alignment and share the same line of sight. If we were to ask, "What do you see?" the contestant could say, "The front sight." But on the same plane would the more distant bull's-eye. Thus one "meaning" or vision is true of all three focal points

In this way, the proud and audacious Babylonian king's braggadocio and his subsequent humiliation similarly describe Satan's desire to rise to equality with God and his subsequent descent in ignominious shame and disgrace. The king of Babylon had boasted in his exalted terms:

---

3. For more details, see my article, "Psalm 72: An Historical and Messianic Current Example of Antiochene Hermeneutical Theoria," *Journal of Evangelical Theological Society* 52/2 (June 2009): 257–70. See also my work *Introduction to Biblical Hermeneutics* (Grand Rapids: Zondervan, 2009), 158.

"I will ascend to the heavens;
I will raise my throne
Above the stars of God;
I will sit enthroned on the mount of assembly,
On the utmost heights of Mount Zaphon.
I will ascend above the tops of the clouds;
I will make myself like the Most High" (Isa. 14:13–14).

The Hebrew word translated as "morning star" ("How have you fallen from heaven, morning star, son of the dawn!" Isa. 14:12) then describes at once both the Babylonian ruler (in history) and Satan (in the past and future). The idea that Satan was intended by this term is found as early as the early Christian writer Tertullian of Carthage (AD 160–220), who wrote prolifically in Latin. In the later Latin translation of the Bible (the Vulgate, AD 405), the Hebrew word for "morning star" (*helel*) was rendered as "Lucifer," which translation also made its way into the Authorized Version (KJV) in 1611.

The text says that he (the king) was cast down to earth, apparently just as Satan was cast out of heaven ("You have been cast down to the earth, you who once laid low the nations!" Isa. 14:12c-d) . The transgression committed by both the king of Babylon and Satan was that they "said in [their] heart[s], to emphasize the point once again, 'I will ascend to heaven; I will raise my throne above the stars of God; I will sit enthroned on the mount of assembly, on the utmost heights of the sacred mountain. I will ascend above the tops of the clouds; I will make myself like the Most High.' But you are brought down to the grave, to the depths of the pit" (Isa. 14:13–15).

It is true that Ugaritic tablets from Ras Shamra, Syria (discovered in 1929), contain some of the same words used in Isaiah 14, such as "morning star" (*helel*), "dawn" (*shahar*), and "sacred mountain" (*zaphon*); but no specific myth has been found that matches the reality that is found in Isaiah 14.

So we argue for a *single* meaning to this text; because of its hyperbolic use of words, however, it has a *multiple* identification yet with a single meaning that embraces at one and the same time both the Babylonian king and Satan.

Ezekiel 28:12–19 is very similar to Isaiah 14:12–15. It is also a sarcastic mockery of the King of Tyre, who likewise had an exaggerated view of himself and his accomplishments.[4] Tyre was an extremely wealthy commercial trade cen-

---

4.   His name was Ithobaal II, also known as Ethbaal II or Ittobaal II.

ter, which Ezekiel portrays as gloating over the fall of Jerusalem (Ezek. 26:2). Ezekiel foretells the destruction of the city of Tyre by Nebuchadnezzar of Babylon (26:7–14); yet suddenly in the midst of Ezekiel's prophecy (v. 12) the pronouns change from the third person masculine singular ("he") to 3rd person plural pronouns ("they").

Here two events, one near and one far, are both fulfillments of Ezekiel's prophecy. "Nebuchadnezzar . . . besieged Tyre for thirteen years (585–572 bc), but the precise historical facts of its outcome are still unclear. He evidently did not conquer the city, but it may have surrendered conditionally to him. Apparently both Tyre and Sidon surrendered to Nebuchadnezzar, based on a fragmentary Babylonian administrative document which mentions the kings of Tyre and Sidon as receiving rations from the royal Babylonian household."[5] It would take Alexander the Great, two hundred and fifty years later, to take the city, enslave the survivors, and raze it to the ground. This Alexander the Great did, as prophesied here, by "demolish[ing] your fine houses and throw[ing] your stones, timber and rubble into the [Mediterranean} Sea" (Ezek. 26:12c-d). Thus Alexander built a causeway one-half mile out into the sea and eventually took the city now located on an island in the Mediterranean Sea!

In chapter 28, Ezekiel returns to the lament of the fall of Tyre with hyperbolic language in Ezekiel 28:13, 14, 16.

> "You were in Eden,
> The garden of God,
> Every precious stone adorned you. . . .
> You were anointed as a guardian cherub,
> For so I ordained you.
> You were on the holy mount of God;
> you walked among the fiery stones.
> So I drove you in disgrace from the mount of God,
> And I expelled you, guardian cherub."

Thus the king of Tyre, uses language that is also descriptive of Satan. He is described as being "in Eden" (Ezek. 28:13) and characterized by exceptional beauty,

---

5. Gary Byers, "The Biblical Cities of Tyre and Sidon," *Bible and Spade,* January 26, 2010, http://www.biblearchaeology.org/post/2010/01/26/the-biblical-cities-of-tyre-and-sidon.aspx (accessed March 11, 2015).

wisdom, and purity (28:12). All sorts of precious stones adorned him on the day
he was created, but then God "expelled" him from "the mount of God" (28:16)
and "threw [him] down to the earth" (28:17). Such descriptions seem also to fit
Satan's expulsion from heaven. The result of this expulsion is that all the nations
were "appalled" at this sudden lose of prosperity and position (28:19), and both
the king of Tyre and Satan came to "a horrible end" and were "no more" (28:19b).

Conclusion

Satan is not presented as one of the main characters of the Old Testament,
but it is clear that, from the very beginning in the Garden of Eden, his hand was
evident even though his name was not always highlighted. In order to keep any
incipient dualism or polytheism from rearing its head, his name is held back in
reserve in the Old Testament, but his work is often seen nevertheless.

Once the hyperbolic forms of the laments in Isaiah 14 and Ezekiel 28 are
identified, it is also possible to have a record of Satan's early fall from his position
of prominence to his present work of being the accuser of the brethren. Where
Satan seems to be strong, Yahweh the Lord was and always is stronger and sovereign over the situations of life and history.

So did God create Satan? If Satan was indeed an angel of light and a heavenly
being as the Bible indicates, he was a part of God's creation. We can deduce from
this that Satan was originally "good" in the same sense that God pronounced all
of His creation to be good. As Genesis 3 portrays Satan's activities in the Garden
of Eden and as Isaiah and Ezekiel portray his character, it is clear that God is not
the author or cause of Satan's rebellion nor is He the originator of evil. Satan's
judgment by God and his expulsion from heaven is evidence of God's moral or-
dering of the universe; and while God does, for His own purposes, permit Satan
to exist, Satan is not like God-like in his power and knowledge. God's ultimate
judgment of Satan will end all of the deceiver's pretensions of power, and his
final end will be the lake of fire (Rev. 20:10).

Discussion Questions

1. What liabilities and possible errors can develop from an overemphasis
   on the demonic, the magical occultic practices as Deuteronomy 18:14–
   22 warned?

2. What biblical texts seem to point to a heavenly assembly and to Satan's participation in that council? What do you make of these texts?

3. What does Jesus' line of argument in John 10:34–36 seem to teach about the identity of the "sons of God?"

4. Does Genesis 3:15 refer to Satan in the term "The Serpent"? What evidence supports this thesis and what evidence rules against it?

5. If Satan appears in the prologue to Job (1:6–12; 2:1–6), why is nothing said about him in the epilogue of Job?

6. Is Satan's fall from heaven described in Isaiah 14:12–15 and Ezekiel 28:12–19? If so, what supports this view and if not, why is it not proper to see him in those passages?

8

The God Who Is Omniscient or the God Who Doesn't Know the Future?

Question: Is the God of the Old Testament the God who knows the future or the God who has left the future open and unknown to himself?

In 1980 Richard Rice began a debate on the omniscience of God that later became known as "The Openness of God" or "Open Theism" position.[1] In part, it was a reopening of the older debate on predestination and free will that had usually been paired off as a debate between Calvinism or Arminianism. Thus, in some ways, the issue became one of trying to justify God's sovereign immutability with human responsibility and to understand what amount of free will or choice belongs human beings.

As this debate has now taken shape, classical theists and open theists agree that God knows everything. But where they disagree is over the *extent* of that "everything." For classical theists, who follow that ancient classical theist St. Augustine, God's knowledge includes everything past, present, and future. Augustine declared that if God did not know everything, then he could not be God.[2] In other words, it would be impossible to define God without the divine attribute of omniscience.

---

1. Richard Rice, *The Openness of God* (Nashville: Review and Herald, 1980).
2. Augustine, *City of God*, 5.9.

Contrariwise, John Sanders, representing the Open Theist viewpoint, announced that "God knows all the past and present, but there is no exhaustively definite future for God to know."[3] Therein lies the heart of the question: Does God know or does he not know everything about the future? As this discussion continued, it became clear that the debate really revolved around which biblical texts are given hermeneutical priority in formulating the doctrine of omniscience. What was an interpreter to do about those texts where God seems to have had a change of mind? Are these texts to be taken as being a literal change in the divine mind or were they figurative expressions? Were these anthropomorphic expressions describing God as if he were a human being and that he had learned things about the future, just as human beings learn things about the future? In order to get a handle on this issue, we will need to look at four types of biblical texts that can help us gain a perspective on God's relationship to the future. Examining these texts should help us answer some of the questions associated with this issue.

The Use of "Perhaps" in Divine Speech

On at least five occasions the word "perhaps" (Hebrew, `ulay`) is used in speeches that are attributed to God. When the same expression is used in human speech, it normally means some kind of uncertainty about the future, but with a slight note of hope attached to it as well.

"Perhaps" Statements Made in Regards to Humans

First, let's look at some examples of usages of this word in regards to persons (emphasis added in Scripture quotes below). Exodus 32:30 records Moses using this term in addressing the nation of Israel:

> The next day Moses said to the people, "You have committed a great sin. But now I will go up to the LORD; **perhaps** I can make atonement for your sin" (Exod. 32:30).

A similar usage is seen in the prophet Amos 5:15, where the prophet is speaking:

> Hate evil, love good; maintain justice in the courts. **Perhaps** the LORD God Almighty will have mercy on the remnant of Joseph.

---

3. John Sanders. *The God Who Risks* (Downers Grove, IL: InterVarsity Press, 1998), 129.

In these instances, nothing was promised except a hope that in the mercy of God, relief might be found. The note of uncertainty is certainly present from a human point of view, but the question is this: is that true also of the divine point of view?

"Perhaps" Statements Made by God

There are at least five instances where God used the word *perhaps* as well. For the first example, note the following by the prophet Ezekiel:

> The word of the LORD came to me: "Son of man . . . pack your belongings for exile and in the daytime, as they watch, set out and go from where you are to another place. **Perhaps** they will understand, though they are a rebellious house" (Ezek. 12:1–3).

In a similar manner, the prophet Jeremiah was told:

> This is what the LORD says: Stand in the courtyard of the LORD's house, and speak to all the people. . . . **Perhaps** they will listen, and each will turn from his evil way. Then I will relent and not bring on them the disaster I was planning because of the evil they have done (Jer. 26:2–3).

In another text concerning Jeremiah we note:

> This word came to Jeremiah from the LORD, "Take a scroll and write on it all the words I have spoken to you concerning Israel. . . . **Perhaps** when the people of Judah hear about every disaster I plan to inflict on them, each of them will turn from his wicked way. . . . **Perhaps** they will bring their petition before the LORD, and each one will turn from his wicked ways, for the anger and wrath pronounced against this people by the LORD are great" (Jer. 36:1–3, 7).

Even in the case of the hostile Babylon, God has a "perhaps" for them as well:

> Babylon will suddenly fall and be broken. Wail over her! Get balm for her pain; **perhaps** she can be healed (Jer. 51:8).

Some commentators have incorrectly concluded that passages that use a divine *perhaps* show that God is "uncertain" as to how the people will respond in the future to the words spoken by the prophets; however, God being God, that is an unlikely conclusion considering how he is described elsewhere and who he is in his person. The psalmist says in Psalms 94:11 that "The LORD knows the thoughts of man; he knows that they are futile." So how could the responses of humans, good or bad, be a surprise or be unknown to God when he knows all the thoughts of mortals? Therefore, how can these *perhaps* statements be explained apart from a knowledge vacuum in the divine being? Do they really indicate that God is uncertain about what is going to happen? Did the Lord actually believe that the people would respond favorably to his word, but then was disappointed with what they did? But first, let's look at another category—the conditional sentence in divine speech.

The Conditional Sentences of Divine Speech

There is another class of "perhaps" statements that parallel the passages that have been examined already: the conditional sentences in divine speech. While conditional sentences are used in Hebrew in a variety of ways, we will focus on the ones that use the Hebrew particle *'im* ("if") with the imperfect [4] form of the verb in the first clause. For example, in Jeremiah 7:5–7 warns, "**If you really change** your ways and your actions, . . . then I will let you live in this place." Or put in its negative form: "**If you do not listen** to the words of my servants the prophets, . . . then I will make this house like the house of Shiloh and this city an object of cursing among all the nations of the earth."

Some wonder what it was that God knew at the moment he gave these conditional prophecies. If God knew that there was no way the Judeans were going to respond as he wished, was he not therefore holding out a false hope to them? How, on that basis, could it have been a valid offer?

In other cases God held out both positive and negative options such as is seen in Jeremiah 22:4–5:

> For **if you are careful** to carry out these commands, then kings who sit on David's throne will come through the gates of this palace, riding in chariots and on horses. . . . But if you do not

---

4. The imperfect form of the Hebrew verb is used to indicate continuous, ongoing action.

obey these commands, declares the LORD, I swear by myself
that this palace will become a ruin.

Some protest that if both options were to be fully open to the kings addressed in Jeremiah 22:4–5, it would be unnecessary for God to fully know
what the future held since it could go either way. Or, if the negative judgment
was the one God knew would be exacted, then the offer was not a genuine
offer for the kings to respond to. If this objection were true, then the Old
Testament view on God's omniscience would need to have a more limited
definition.

Divine Consultation on the Future

God announced to his prophet Amos: "Surely the Sovereign LORD does
nothing without revealing his plan to his servants the prophets" (Amos 3:7).
However, this must not be seen as a binding restraint on God or a declaration
of a closed future. While he reveals to the prophet what the future holds, it is
against the teaching of other parts of Scripture to say that the future remains
locked up and already determined with no provision made for a human responsibility or for a change in one's action.

On two occasions, God reveals what he is going to do in the future. On
those same two occasions, however, the prophet Amos prayed and God re-
scinded his planned judgment in response to the prophet's prayer:

> This is what the Sovereign LORD showed me: He was prepar-
> ing swarms of locusts after the king's share had been harvested
> and just as the second crop was coming up. When they had
> stripped the land clean, I cried out, "Sovereign LORD, forgive!
> How can Jacob survive? He is so small." So the LORD relented.
> "This will not happen," the LORD said (Amos 7:1–3).

Again, in the second prayer by the prophet, he prayed:

> This is what the Sovereign LORD showed me: The Sovereign
> LORD was calling for judgment by fire; it dried up the great
> deep and devoured the land. Then I cried out, "Sovereign
> LORD, I beg you, stop! How can Jacob survive? He is so small."

So the LORD relented. "This will not happen either," the Sovereign LORD said (Amos 7:4–6).

Surely these two examples alone show that the judgment of God on Israel, once announced to the prophet, was not irrevocable. Yahweh cannot be depicted as a frozen immobility incapable of changing if he can change on principle and with full regard to his character. He is a living person, and as such he can and does respond whenever people genuinely change. The same prophecy that gave the judgment also allowed for the intervention and advocacy of the prophet's prayers almost up to the last moment. In fact, one of the tasks of a prophet was precisely just that: a mediatorial role of praying for the people and urging them to repent and turn around from the direction they were going in of opposing and resisting God. But things can turn desperate, for at one point, Jeremiah was also told: "So, do not pray for this people, nor offer any plea or petition for them; do not plead with me, for I will not listen to you" (Jer. 7:16). This command was repeated in Jeremiah 11:14; 14:11; 15:1. Again the point in these texts was that there was no turning away of God's threatened judgment for it was now too late for the people of Judah to repent—they had passed the point of no return. The cup of iniquity had been filled up to the brim by the people of Judah (as happened to Canaan in Genesis 15:16). God would no longer even listen to the prophet's prayer. This prohibition was itself a symbolic action; the point was that time had expired for Judah to show any signs of repentance or any turning around to come back in repentance to Yahweh. Judah had reached the end of the line of God's mercy, patience, and restoration.

But what about other situations? Are there other instances in addition to these examples? Could God change his predicted course of action merely in response to real genuine repentance of mortals? Yes, there is another biblical text that shows that human action could be counted on in determining God's action: Genesis 18:17–21.

> Then the LORD said, "Shall I hide from Abraham what I am about to do? . . . [No] for I have chosen him. . . ." Then the LORD said, "The outcry against Sodom and Gomorrah is so great and their sin is so grievous that I will go down and see if what they have done is as bad as the outcry that has reached me. If not, I will know."

Prior to God's taking action, he makes Abraham aware of what he is about to do for he does not want to hide it from Abraham. But in the timing of God's action, again Sodom and Gomorrah is specifically left open by God to allow for Abraham's involvement in prayer in this crisis and for God to investigate the facts more extensively. He must see and verify these accusations not just for his own satisfaction but also for the sake of mortals so that they might learn from it. God uses real evidence and not just hearsay or the like as the basis for his accusations.

Thereupon, Abraham begins to plead with God: "Will you sweep away the righteous with the wicked?" (v. 23). In the narrative that follows, Abraham suggests that it would be very unlike God, "the Judge of all the earth" not to do what was right (v. 25). And so the bargaining begins as Abraham asks God to spare the cities for the sake of the righteous ones dwelling there, from a group that begins with possibly fifty righteous persons and finally ends with just ten righteous persons living in Sodom and Gomorrah. The question then is: Would those cities be spared if even ten righteous persons could be found in their midst? The divine answer was, Yes. The cities would be spared if just ten righteous persons could be found. Clearly, the fate of those cities rested in part on the behavior of a righteous remnant of just ten persons. Had that number existed, the cities would have been spared God's judgment since the possibility of mercy was divinely promised. Divine judgment could be averted where there was repentance or a sufficient godly remnant present. Thus, for the sake of a few, the many would be given extended days of mercy.

A comparable situation occurred also in Exodus 32:7–14. Moses had been up on Mount Sinai for forty days, but the people despaired of ever seeing Moses again. So they pleaded with Aaron to make them a god. He built for them a golden calf, but when God saw what they had done and how they were now practicing religious prostitution and dancing around the calf idol, he told Moses, "Now leave me alone so that my anger may burn against them and that I may destroy them" (Exod. 32:10). It was as if Moses and perhaps his prayers were not to interfere with the determination of God's judgment on these reprobates.

Many commentators complain that God closed the door to Israel's future and his ancient promises to the patriarchs when he made an alternative offer to Moses that he would make a nation out of him (an offer that clearly excluded Israel from any hope for a future). But Moses intervened on behalf of the people and besought God not to do that. It would seem for the moment that Moses was more merciful than God; but one must recall that it was this same Lord who had made a man like Moses for just such a time as this. We must not, therefore, discount the provision of God in raising up a Moses who would intervene on behalf of the people!

Unconditional and Conditional Prophecies

Moreover, prophecies in the Old Testament exhibit two distinguishable types: unconditional prophecies and conditional prophecies. Unconditional prophecies are those that are connected with our salvation and belong to the Edenic Covenant (Gen. 3:15), the Abrahamic Covenant (Gen. 12:1–3), the Davidic Covenant (2 Sam. 7), or the New Covenant (Jer. 31:31–34). Also included here is the promise of a new heavens and a new earth (Isa. 65–66), and the covenant of the seasons in Noah's day (Gen. 8:21–22). They were all dependent on Yahweh's faithfulness and not at all dependent on Israel's obedience. These prophecies would remain true and abiding even if none of those present generations got to participate in them due to their own lack of faith and belief. Conditional prophecies, on the other hand, had an implicit or an expressed *unless* or an *if* attached to them—". . . unless you repent and turn back to me."

One more illustration of this mediatorial role that God gave to his servants should be noted. In Numbers 14:11–20, a general rebellion broke out in the camp against Moses and Aaron during the wilderness wanderings. The people had had enough desert trekking, so they wanted to choose a new leader and to return back to Egypt, apparently without the leadership of Moses or Aaron. But Moses and Aaron intervened and prayed for these rebels that they might be forgiven, to which God acquiesced as the arguments that Moses raised were honored by God. But the same Lord who had called Moses in the first place was the Lord who had prepared him for this situation as well—he was to stand in the gap between the rebellious and the forgiving Lord as a mediator.

The Divine Question

Another type of examination about the future comes in various questions that God asks. In some of these questions, it appears as if God is struggling and appears to be unable to decide which course of action to take. Consider these examples:

> What can I do with you, Ephraim? What can I do with you, Judah? Your love is like the morning mist, like the early dew that disappears (Hos. 6:4).

Later in his prophecy, the prophet Hosea records what appears at first to be an exasperated and bewildered Lord who asks:

> How can I give you up, Ephraim? How can I hand you over,
> Israel? How can I treat you like Adamah? How can I make you
> like Zeboiim? My heart is changed within me; all my compas-
> sion is aroused. I will not carry out my fierce anger, nor will I
> turn and devastate Ephraim. For I am God, and not man—the
> Holy One among you (Hos. 11:8–9).

Even if this is regarded as metaphorical language, it must have some link-
age with reality—so what is the connection? It is not that God does not have
the resources to know what it is he can do or what he is to do in these situations. He knows, but the depths of human language is extended to its limits
as God attempts to show the sheer agony of carrying out a decision that
he would rather not carry out if only his people obeyed him. In no way do
these questions signal an indecisiveness or a hesitancy to face the future. It is
not that Yahweh does not have the resources or mental capabilities to know
what to do. Nor is it a case where he vacillates between two or more alternative ways of handling the situation, unable to choose between them. Instead,
these questions are indications that the Lord takes into his confidence his
prophet. They reflect a conversation that is on-going and a deep desire to
see a different outcome than what the situation seems to be headed towards,
given the present state of things. Yahweh reveals himself as a God who shares
things about himself and makes himself vulnerable to his prophets and to the
people these prophets must communicate with. In this way, the people can
clearly see the agony and hurt that God experiences as he begs them through
the prophets to reverse their course of action and to repent of their evil and
sinful ways. There is also the hope that seems implicit here that knowing
about such suffering on the part of God will lead the people all the more rap-
idly to repentance. In fact, in Hosea again, after Yahweh has announced an
impending judgment on Israel, God decides to "go back to [his] place until
they admit their guilt. And they will seek [his] face; in their misery they will
earnestly seek [him]" (Hos. 5:15).

Rhetorical Questions

Other questions posed by God compare the present more with the past than
they do with the future. While they could be interpreted as mere rhetorical questions, others list them as "disputational speeches." God directly asks his people:

Have I been a desert to Israel or a land of darkness? Why do my people say, 'We are free to roam; we will come to you no more?' (Jer. 2:31).

The desert, of course, was a most inhospitable place, as Jeremiah 2:6 recalled; it was a place no one wanted to return to. But that was why God asked his people in effect, "Is that how you think of me?"—a place that is dark, foreboding and inhospitable?" Or to put the question as Jeremiah 2:5 phrased it: "What fault did your fathers find in me? Why have you forsaken me and replaced me with other gods?"

Jeremiah asked Yahweh's question once again in Jeremiah 8:5: "*Why* then have these people turned away? *Why* does Jerusalem always turn away? They cling to deceit; they refuse to return." It is not as if God is unable to explain, however, the actions of his people. Rather, in his use of "why?" (Hebrew, *maddua'*) an accusatory meaning is intended, not an intent to signal an absence of divine knowledge. This "why" appears in Jeremiah's prophecy frequently, as seen in Jeremiah 8:19; 13:22; 14:19; 26:9; and 32:3. The point is that even though God knows exactly what has prompted this nation to take such an opposite course of action, it seems to make no sense, given all the advantages and gifts God has showered on them.

The Omniscience of God

While it is true that Scripture does not very often directly refer to God's omniscience, it cannot be said that it is altogether lacking either. In Job 37:16 the young Elihu describes God as being "perfect in knowledge" (even though Elihu made the same claim for himself in Job 36:4 which reduces the credibility of his testimony!). However, the most direct statement can be found in 1 John 3:20: "For God is greater than our hearts, and he knows everything."

Most, however, go to Psalm 139:1–6 to describe what divine omniscience is. The psalmist David begins:

O Lord, you have searched me and you know me. You know when I sit and when I rise; you perceive my thoughts from afar. You discern my going out and my lying down; you are familiar with all my ways. Before a word is on my tongue you know it completely, O Lord. You hem me in—behind and before; you

have laid your hand upon me. Such knowledge is too wonder-
ful for me, too lofty for me to attain.

All attempts to reduce what is claimed in this psalm to merely some form of
a divine investigation to discover what needs to be known about life and mortals
misses the point. Instead, it claims that nothing about us escapes the knowledge
that God has of everything in his universe. To overlook the fact that God even
knows what we are going to say, even before we say it, cannot be explained as one
attempted to interpret it: "God hears every word I say." That is certainly true,
but it reduces what is claimed here by miles. God knows even what I am *going*
to say, not only what it is that I have said!

More on Conditional Prophecies

Is it true that in some cases God declared what would happen in the future
only to be second-guessed and outmaneuvered by mere mortals who by their actions forced a change in the divine plans as well? What this question anticipates
is the existence in Scripture of a special category of what we call conditional
prophecies. The fulfillment of these predictions is dependent and contingent on
the actions of men and women.

The difficulty in understanding this category is caused by an inadequate
view of God and with a failure to understand the conditions contained either directly or indirectly in these prophecies. To begin with, God is not some change-
less impersonal force, who is rigidly incapable of responding in a vital way to
changes in others. Such an impersonal view of God the Father, or his Son, Our
Lord Jesus Christ, is outside the boundaries of Scripture. Our God is a living
person; he can and does respond.

For example, Yahweh's words to Pharaoh document the possibility of a
change in divine action when mortals change. This change in God's actions happens yet does not induce a change in God's qualities, characteristics, attributes,
or nature. God says:

For by now I could have stretched out my hand and struck you
and your people with a plague that would have wiped you off
the earth. But I have raised you up for this very purpose, that
I might show you my power and that my name might be proclaimed in all the earth (Exod. 9:15).

It is not that one of God's standards, his nature, or his being has changed. Rather, in keeping with what we know of other living persons (who can change their actions when a person who has offended them turns and repents), so God as a living person can likewise change in his actions when there is a basis for doing so while retaining the stability of his character and nature.

This can be seen in the life of King Zedekiah. In Jeremiah 38:17–18, two alternatives were put before him:

> If you surrender to the officers of the king of Babylon, your life will be spared and this city will not be burned down; you and your family will live. But if you will not surrender to the officers of the king of Babylon, this city will be handed over to the Babylonians and they will burn it down; you yourself will not escape from their hands.

Unfortunately, Zedekiah chose the second option and found the prophecy was true. In this case the conditions were clearly spelled out with two ways a person could go. These conditions are not always spelled out so distinctly as they were here, but we can see the full form of the condition in this example:

Not long after this prediction, Jeremiah gave another choice to the people who were left in the land of Judah and were spared the pains of going into captivity along with the majority of their countrymen. In Jeremiah 42:10–16 God declared:

> If you stay in this land [of Judah], I will build you up and not tear you down. . . . However, if you say, "We will not stay in this land," and so disobey the LORD your God, and if you say, "No, we will go and live in Egypt, where we will not see war or hear the trumpet or be hungry for bread". . . then the sword you fear will overtake you into Egypt, and there, and the famine you dread will follow into Egypt, and there you will die.

Once again, the people made the wrong choice. But here was another conditional prophecy of the Lord. It too came true!

There were times, however, where the "unless," or the condition statement, was not explicitly stated. Isaiah's message to King Hezekiah was pretty straightforward, offering no conditions or options: "This is what the LORD says; 'Put your house in order, because you are going to die, you will not recover'" (2 Kings 20:1). Everything seemed already fixed and predetermined: Hezekiah was going to die, period. However, Hezekiah turned his face to the wall and prayed as he wept bitterly. Before the prophet Isaiah had left the palace courtyard, the Lord instructed him to return and go back to Hezekiah to give a new word to him. "This is what the LORD, the God of your father David, says, 'I have heard your prayer and seen your tears; I will heal you. . . . I will add fifteen years to your life'" (2 Kings 20:5–6). God changed in his actions (but not his nature), because Hezekiah had prayed!

The clearest statement of this principle can be found in Jeremiah 18:7–10, which reads:

> If at any time I announce that a nation or kingdom is to be uprooted, torn down and destroyed, and if that nation I warned repents of its evil, then I will relent and not inflict on it the disaster I had planned. And if at another time I announce that a nations or kingdom is to be built up and planted, and if it does evil in my sight and does not obey me, then I will reconsider the good I had intended to do for it.

Note that this statement is already put in a *principlized form*, for it is not addressed to any single nation but is put in its broadest terms possible and is operative for all nations on earth. These are nations that have the blessing of God on them if they repent, just as there are nations on earth that are under the judgment of God if they refuse to turn back to him. In the end it will all depend on how each nation responds to the word of God. Even those who are without a prophet or declarer of the truth are still without excuse as Paul argued in Romans 1–2, for what can be known of God is already written on their conscience so that they either accuse or excuse themselves!

It is the application of this principle that made the prophet Jonah so hesitant to go to Nineveh. Even though God's message to Jonah contained no conditions in it; nevertheless, he knew that if they ever repented, then the judgment he announced on behalf of God would be averted for that period of time. And that is what happened, much to the chagrin of Jonah. Nineveh repented, and the forty days came and went without any judgment in sight, until more than a century later in the days of the prophet Nahum.

What is true of nations is also true of individuals as well. For example, when the prophet Elijah threatened King Ahab of Israel with a predetermined judgment ("In the place where dogs licked up Naboth's blood, dogs will lick up your blood—yes, yours!" 1 Kings 21:19), Ahab was properly sobered by this stern announcement. The king tore his clothes in grief, fasted, and put on sackcloth and went about meekly before the Lord (1 Kings 21:27).

Such a complete change in Ahab brought a corresponding change in the actions that God would take, for it was he who informed Ahab, "Because [you have] humbled [yourself], I will not bring this disaster in [your] day" (1 Kings 21:29). Elijah never mentioned that there was a built-in condition to his prediction of judgment, but Ahab acted on the presumption that such a condition might be the case, given the fact that God's character is one of grace and mercy. And so it was! The same individualized application of this principle can be seen also in Ezekiel 33:13–16.

In some cases, the effect of responding positively to the word of God in repentance has the effect of delaying the fulfillment of the prediction. This can be seen in the case of young King Josiah in 2 Kings 22:19–20. When the "Book of the Law" was found during a cleaning up of the temple, the king's humble response to the word of God brought this response from Huldah the prophet:

> Because your heart was responsive and you humbled yourself
> before the Lord when you heard what I have spoken against
> this place and its people, . . . therefore I will gather you to your
> fathers, and you will be buried in peace. Your eyes will not see
> all the disaster I am going to bring on this place.

King Josiah found the Book of the Law in 621 BC, but he died in 609 BC, just before Daniel and his three friends were taken to Babylon in 605 BC; before Ezekiel was taken there in 598 BC; and before the city of Jerusalem was destroyed by fire and the people carted off to Babylon in 586 BC. Because Josiah repented and humbled himself before God, the threatened judgment was delayed and put on an altered schedule, even though it eventually did come after Josiah was gone.

Another instance of this same type of delay in a threatened word of disaster came in Micah 3:12. This eighth-century BC prophet's word had a good effect on King Hezekiah and many who lived in his day, for they responded positively to Micah's message. In fact, so remarkable was this prediction that Jeremiah made a favorable mention of this word a century later in Jeremiah 26:18–19: "Did not Hezekiah fear the LORD and seek his favor [when Micah had said], 'Zion will be plowed like a field, Jerusalem will become a heap of rubble, the temple hill a mound overgrown with thickets']? And did not the LORD relent, so that he did not bring the disaster he pronounced against them"?

Once again, the king's repentance and the repentance of those who humbled themselves before the Lord with him, obviated for the time being the fulfillment of what again proved to be a conditional prophecy from Micah's time in the eighth century BC until the seventh and sixth-centuries BC.

Sequential Prophecies

In addition to conditional and unconditional prophecies, there is a third type of prophecies in the Bible: sequential prophecies. Since these are not as numerous as the other types, we will illustrate this type with the prophecy against Tyre in Ezekiel 26.

The prophet Ezekiel spoke by order of the Lord, predicting that "many nations" would come up against Tyre (Ezek. 26:3). Nebuchadnezzar came first and in verses 4–11 he is explicitly named and the pronouns used are uniformly "he" and "his" are used as the passage continues to talk about his attempted capture of Tyre. However, he was denied an absolute victory as the Tyrians moved off shore to the island part of the city one-half mile offshore in the Mediterranean Sea.[5] After thirteen years Nebuchadnezzar had to break off his siege of Tyre and give up on conquering these people.

However, Ezekiel 26:11 suddenly shifts from the third singular pronoun, referring to Nebuchadnezzar, to another nation who came against Tyre almost 250 years later. This was Alexander the Great, who did just what verse 11 said he would do centuries before he came: "they will break down your walls and demolish your fine homes and throw your stones, timber and rubble *into the sea*." Alexander also, at first frustrated by the Tyrians, finally scrapped up what was left of the mainland city of Tyre and dumped it into the Mediterranean, then built a causeway a half mile out into the Mediter-

---

5. Tyre consisted of a walled, shoreline city and an island city just offshore. During the siege of Alexander the Great in 322 BC, residents abandoned the mainland city and retreated to the island city that was also fortified. Alexander tore down the onshore city and used the debris to build a causeway to the island, where his battering rams quickly breached the walls and his army took the island city.

ranean Sea and marched his army on this newly built land bridge out to take the island city of Tyre.

Thus, while the prophecy was not fulfilled all at once, it predicted that "many nations" would be involved before it all was over. Thus, this prophecy happened in a sequence of events.

Conclusion

All prophetic utterances, then, are not conditional. The covenants already mentioned—the Edenic, Abrahamic, Davidic, and the New Covenant, plus the new heavens and new earth—were matters that "the Lord has sworn to [by himself] and [he] will not change his mind" (Ps. 110:4). But there is every indication that the same Lord issued words of warning and judgment with the prospect that some would see the need for change. God will then issue his change or delay the judgment to another, later generation, which in turn repeats some of the same acts of rebellion and disobedience and refuses to turn back to God.

God is indeed omniscient and all-knowing in all his ways and deeds. A careful study does not bear out the claims of "Open Theism," or the assertion that God has deliberately limited his knowledge of the future to make room for the freedom of human choice. There still is a place for human choice, but it is calculated within the omniscience of God for the past, present, and future.

Discussion Questions

1. What is the position of "Open Theism" and how did it begin?

2. Does the use of the word "perhaps" signal some uncertainty to the mind of God about the future?

3. Which prophecies in the Bible are unconditional? What does this label mean about those prophecies?

4. Give some examples of prophecies that are conditional. But how can any prophecies about the future be conditional when Amos 3:7 is so certain that the Lord will do nothing in the future without revealing his plan to his servants?

5. How are we to interpret statements about God not knowing what course of action to take, when he is omniscient?

6. What are the best texts for the omniscience of God?

9

The God Who Elevates Women or the God Who Devalues Women?[1]

Question: *Has the God of the Old Testament subordinated women to men or has he given men and women equal status and authority?*

If we all approach the text of Scripture with each having his or her own framework of understanding (even when we share a view of the Bible that it is inerrant and true in all it affirms and teaches), is there any hope that we can ever reach a "correct" or "objectively valid" interpretation,[2] especially on passages that are as sensitive as those that deal with the place and privilege of women in the body of Christ? Surely, no one particular set of presuppositions is to be favored in and of itself over any other set of presuppositions as the proper preparation for understanding a text. And no one starts with a *tabula rasa*, a blank slate of impressions, experiences, and opinions. So does this mean we are hopelessly deadlocked with no possibility for a resolution on this important question?

Even though evangelicals do argue about some issues (despite acknowledging that we all begin with a certain number of presuppositions), this does not demolish the possibility of reaching a biblically supported interpretation.

---

1. This adapted article first appeared in the *Priscilla Papers* 19.2 (2005): 5–11, under the title "Correcting Caricatures: The Biblical Teaching on Women," by Walter C. Kaiser, Jr.
2. I am indebted to a marvelous recent work by Thomas Howe, *Objectivity in Biblical Interpretation* (Longwood, FL: Advantage Books, 2004), for the argument that follows.

Our pre-understandings are subject to change in light of the evidence, and therefore they can and should be altered by the text of Scripture and the facts of the situation. Just as one must not involve one's self in a hopeless contradiction by declaring that "absolutely, there are no absolutes," so in the same manner, to declare, "Objectively, there are no objective or correct meanings possible for interpreting a passage of Scripture" is to decry exactly what is being affirmed.

The way out of this quandary of both the relativist or the perspectivalist (i.e., one that only reflects one's perspective) conundrum is to identify the presence of those aspects of thought that are self-evident first principles of thought that transcend every perspective and act the same way for all people, in all cultures, all times, and all settings.[3]

This is not to say that a correct or an objective interpretation is always reached in every attempted interpretation. But for those who accept that the God who has created human beings and has given us the gift of language when he made us in his own image, it is not a stretch to say that a "correct" and "objective" understanding is possible for subsequent readers of the earlier revelation of God. The God who made the world is the same God who made our minds, thus a direct connection between my mind and the world is possible. To deny objectivity would be self-defeating, for it would again reduce itself to a violation of the law of non-contradiction. Accordingly, there is real hope for realizing an objective meaning and deciding between various truth claims and even between differing perspectives and different worldviews.[4]

All of this is a preface to the following discussion for some Christians have grown so weary of this discussion that they have just given up and decided that nothing more can be said that will move others from their entrenched positions. As evangelicals, however, we must neither surrender to the status quo of a multiplicity of competing interpretations nor reject simply out of hand an honest discussion of the key points of Scripture on these matters even if we disagree with the discussion on absolutes in the previous paragraphs. All valid interpretations will stand both the test of challenges as well as the test of time. So, for one more time, let us look at the Scripture's teaching on the value and gifts God has given to women because Scripture, after all, should be the only and final arbiter for evangelical interpreters.

---

3. Howe, *Objectivity*, 463.
4. Ibid., 465.

1. Genesis 2:18 teaches that the woman possessed "power" or "strength" corresponding to the man.

Adam was regarded by his Creator as incomplete and deficient as he lived at first without the benefit of a proper counterpart or without a community of persons. God said, "It is not good for the man to be alone" (Gen. 2:18); or, as Ecclesiastes 4:9–11 expresses it, "Two are better than one." Accordingly, in order to end man's loneliness, God formed for Adam [a] "suitable helper," or at least that is the way most have rendered the Hebrew word `ezer in Genesis 2:18.

Now there is nothing pejorative about the translation "helper," for the same word is used for God and is also variously translated as "strength" as in "He is your shield and *helper*" in Deuteronomy 33:29 and 33:26 (`ezer here equals "strength").

But recently R. David Freedman[5] has argued quite convincingly that the Hebrew word `ezer is a combination of two older Hebrew/Canaanite roots, one `ezer, meaning "to rescue" or "to save" and `gezer meaning "to be strong" (using their verbal forms for the moment). The difference between the two initial letters that spell these two words is in the first letter that today is somewhat silent in pronunciation and comes in the Canaanite alphabet about where the letter "o" comes in the order of the English alphabet. The initial Hebrew letter `g, or `ghayyin, fell together with another sign in the Hebrew alphabet and was represented by the one sign ` or `ayyin for both of the former letters.

However, we do know that both letters were originally pronounced separately, for their sounds are preserved in the "g" sound still preserved in English today in place names such as *Gaza* or *Gomorrah*, both of which are now spelled in Hebrew with the same letter, `ayyin. Ugaritic, ancient Canaanite language, shares about sixty percent of its vocabulary with Hebrew. Formerly, it distinguished between the letters `ghayyin and `ayyin in its alphabet of thirty letters (it represents the first alphabetic language of the world from around 1500 to 1200 BC). It seems that somewhere around 1500 BC the two phonemes, or units of sound, merged into one written unit, or grapheme, and thus the two verbal roots merged into one. Moreover, the Hebrew word `ezer appears twenty-one times in the Old Testament, often in parallelism with words denoting "strength" or "power," thereby suggesting that two individual words were still being repre-

---

5. R. David Freedman, "Woman, a Power Equal to Man," *Biblical Archaeology Review* 9 (1983): 56–58.

sented under a single common spelling of an initial unit of sound. Thus the Hebrew word `ezer, meaning "helper or strength," might also be the same spelling
for the earlier Canaanite word `ghezzer, meaning "power." Therefore, I believe it
is best to consider the translation of Genesis 2:18 as "I will make [the women] a
power [or a strength] corresponding to the man."

The proof for this rendering seems to be indicated in 1 Corinthians 11:10
where Paul argued, "For this reason, a woman ought to have power [or author-
ity] on her head." The Greek word *exousia*, as used by Paul in 1 Corinthians,
consistently means "authority" or "power," which would agree with the rendering given above for Genesis 2:18. Moreover, *exousia* is never used in the passive
sense, but only in the active sense (1 Cor. 7:37; 8:9; 9:4, 5). But in the one of
the strangest twists in translation history, this one word was rendered "a veil, a
symbol of authority" on her head by most of the earlier versions! But as Katherine C. Bushnell demonstrated in the early twentieth century, the substitution of
"veil" for "power" goes all the way back to the Gnostic teacher Valentinus, who
founded a sect named after himself in Alexandria, Egypt, sometime between
AD 140 and his death in 160. His native tongue was Coptic, and in Coptic the
word for "power" and the word for "veil" bore a close resemblance in sound and
in print: *ouershishi*, meaning "power, authority," and *ouershoun*, meaning "veil."
Both Clement and Origen also came from Alexandria so they also made the
identical mistake, possibly off the same Coptic manuscripts or from the influence of Valentinus.

This debacle continues right down to our own day. For example, the New
International Translation says "the woman ought to have a *sign of authority* on her
head." Note that the NET, NASB, ESV, NKJV, and NRSV seem to follow the
same path using the word "symbol" rather than "sign." Even though the awful
word "veil" has dropped out of more recent translations, the expanded "sign of
authority" for *exousia* remains stuck in the English text, even though there is no
Greek word representing the word "sign." Or "symbol." But let the word *exousia*
stand as it should, and the question becomes, "Where did Paul find that "power"
or "authority" was placed on the head of a woman? In Genesis 2:18!

So rather than saying a woman is to be a "helper corresponding to the man;"
instead, the text teaches that the woman has been given "authority, strength, or
power" that is "equal to [man's]." The full Hebrew expression is `ezer kenegdo*. If
later Hebrew is of any help here, this second Hebrew word, often translated as
"corresponding to him," is used in later Hebrew to mean "equal to him." Surely,
such a being, equal to him, would assuage Adam's loneliness.

This line of reasoning is also borne out in Genesis 2:23 where Adam says to Eve, "This is now bone of my bones and flesh of my flesh; she shall be called 'woman,' for she was taken out of man." This idiomatic expression points to family closeness, one's own close relative, or, in effect, "my equal."

Finally, woman was never meant to be a "helpmate," no matter which force if given to this word `*ezer*. The Old English "meet" or "suitable to" was adapted into a new English word, "mate." What God had intended, however, was to make a "power" or "strength" who would in every respect "correspond to" the man or even to be "his equal."

2. Genesis 3:16 is not a command for man to rule over the woman, but it is a curse: men, unfortunately, will rule over women.

This text, contrary to popular opinion and repeatedly used in an incorrect appeal for support to 1 Corinthians 14:34 ("[Women] are not allowed to speak, but must be in submission, as the *law* says"), does not demand that men are to take charge of their women and "rule over them." Rather than viewing this as a normative and prescriptive text found in the Mosaic Law and revealed by God, it is in a curse passage that predicts what will happen when women "turn" toward their husbands instead of turning to God. The truth is that as a result of the fall, do not be surprised, women, if men try to "lord" it over you.

The statement in Genesis 3:16 does not have the slightest hint of a normative command or a biblical mandate for men to assume that they are in charge; nor is it a prescriptive command from God by any means. Hebrew grammar does not allow for this text to be rendered as "the man *must* or *shall* rule over you." To demand such a rendering here would be to invite a similar move in Genesis 3:18, where the text would read "the ground *must* produce thorns and thistles for you." If the later were so, then farmers, on the assumption that this is a correct rendering of the text, would need to stop using weed killer or pulling out thorns and thistles since God, on the contrary, demands that the weeds be left in place in the farm. That, of course is silly—and so is the same logic used to render verse 16 in the traditionally understood sense of a command.

Some, of course, will object by saying that Genesis 4:7 has the same construction, where "sin is crouching at your door; it desires to have you, but you must master it" (NIV). The word translated here as "desire" (incorrectly so, as we shall see later) and the verb translated "master" ("to rule") are found both used in

Genesis 3:16. Accordingly, it is alleged that the rendering of Genesis 4:7 seems to validate the traditional rendering of Genesis 3:16.

However, a more preferable rendering of the verb in Genesis 4:7 is to understand that a question is being asked here. The Hebrew particle signaling a question is absent in about one-half of the Hebrew questions in the Bible, as it is here. However, the context and the verb signal that this is a question. Therefore, we would render the last part of Genesis 4:7, "But you, will you rule over it?" (i.e., will you, Cain, rule over the sin that is lingering at the door of your heart? That would allow for the verb to be rendered in its normal way "*will* rule," rather than non-grammatical form of "*must* rule."

So, the traditional move to see the "law" referred to in 1 Corinthians 14:34–35 as the Mosaic Torah is totally without any basis, for the Genesis passage would need to command and mandate husbands to rule over their wives, which it distinctly does not. As we will see later on, there are plenty of places in the Jewish "law" of the Talmud and Mishnah where just such a command does occur, but one is pressed to embarrassment to find any such hint, much less an order, to do such in the Law of Moses or, for that matter, anywhere else in the Old Testament.

3. Genesis 3:16 does not teach that women developed sexual desires or lust for men as a result of the fall.

The translation of Genesis 3:16 has to be one of the oddest stories ever told. It is a travesty of errors, in which one man in particular—an Italian Dominican monk named Pagnino—published his Latin version at Lyons in AD 1528 with the meaning "lust" (rendered from there on out usually as "desire") and thus occasioned a parade of copy-cats who have continued to follow his lead to this very day.

The Hebrew word *teshuqa* is translated only three times in the third-century BC Greek Septuagint,[6] where it is rendered in the two Genesis passages as

---

6. Theodotion's rendering in Greek (c. AD 150) is "turning," as Katherine C. Bushnell explains in her *God's Word to Women*, (often privately printed since the final edition came out in 1923), paragraphs 128–145. However, Symmachus's Greek rendering (late fourth century AD) followed Aquila's suggestion (c. AD 126), rendering it by the Greek word *horme*, "impulse." Aquila, noted Bushnell, was a proselyte to Judaism who followed the Jewish scholars of the second century AD. In the Talmud ((mid-fourth century AD), which is technically not a translation of the Bible, but a listing of traditions, it teaches that there were ten curses pronounced over Eve, and in the fifth, sixth and ninth of these curses, it used the word "lust" to render the

apostrophe, meaning "turning away," and in the Song of Solomon passage as *epistrohe*, meaning "turning to." The Samaritan Pentateuch (whose oldest extant manuscript is from the eleventh century AD) also rendered the two passages as "turning" as did the Old Latin and the Coptic or Bohairic versions (both of which are from early AD 400s), as well as the Ethiopic version of c. AD 500.

Jerome's Latin translation of the Bible, the Vulgate (383–405), under the influence of Jewish rabbis, rendered Genesis 3:16, "Thou shalt be under the power of a husband, and he will rule over thee." And so the history of an error began.

The result was that Pagnino's version appeared later in every English version. But the problem with Pagnino, as with those earlier deviations already representatively noted here, was this: they tended to depend on the rabbis for their sense of this infrequently used word in the Bible instead of depending on the ancient versions of the Scripture such as the Greek Septuagint, the Syriac Peshitto, the Samaritan Pentateuch, the Old Latin, the Coptic versions, and the Ethiopic. But where the rabbis or the Babylonian Talmud was followed, such as Aquila's Greek, Symmachus's Greek, Theodotion's Greek or the Latin Vulgate, preference was given to translation such as "lust," "impulse," "alliance" or the like.

Bushnell concludes her detailed piece of philological and translation detective work by saying, "Of the 28 known renderings [in ancient translations] of *teshuqa*, . . . the word is rendered 'turning' 21 times. In the 7 remaining renderings, only 2 seem to agree; all the others disagree."[7] Even the early church fathers give evidence of knowing no other rendering for this Hebrew word than "turning."

Therefore, let us be done once and for all with any idea that women, since the Fall, have lusted after men so that is why men must control them as best they can. This must be a male fantasy at best or a downright imposition of one's own imagination on the text at worst. Nevertheless, certain interpretive schools of thought grew up around a word with very limited usage in the Scriptures, and therefore the error has persisted.

Eve "turned" from her Lord, and instead placed all her dependency in her husband only to find out that he, too, as a fallen sinner, would take advantage of her and rule over her. Instead of experiencing the norm that God had prescribed,

---

Hebrew word *teshuqa*. Thus, in Origen's *Hexapla* (an eight-column listing of all the variant readings of Scripture he knew about from before AD 240). Aquila's column rendered the word there "coalition," or "alliance," which Bushnell says is not all that an unnatural sense "since Eve is represented as turning from God to form an alliance with her husband."

7. Bushnell, paragraph 139.

it turns out that it is a description of another curse that has fallen on humanity, and women in particular, because of the Fall described in Genesis 3:1–13.

4.   Exodus 38:8 and 1 Samuel 2:22, among other passages, show that women served at the Tabernacle and ministered as prophetesses in the Old Testament.

"Women who served" at the tabernacle in Exodus 38:8 and 1 Samuel 2:22 were too much for the Greek translators of the Septuagint to take, so they changed it to "women who fast." Bushnell quotes a Professor Margoliouth of Oxford as decrying such an idea with the words, "The idea of women in attendance at the Tabernacle is so odious that it has to be got rid of."[8] And so it was gotten rid of in the Authorized Version (KJV) that mistranslated it as "assembled" while other translations substituted "prayed" or "thronged" instead of "served." But there it stood: there were women who served at the tabernacle.

It seems that for these translators, the very idea of women "serving" was too far out of conformity with the "established" idea of female subordination to men. However, what shall we say of Miriam? Miriam is called a "prophetess" in Exodus 15:20 as she led the women in what seems to be antiphonal singing (along with musical instruments and dances) of the song of Moses that the Israelites had just sung (Exod. 15:1–19). In Micah 6:4, she listed as one of the three leaders of the people: "For I brought you up from the land of Egypt and redeemed you from the house of slavery, and I sent before you Moses, Aaron, and Miriam" (ESV). Among the thousands of people who died in the wilderness journey, her importance is highlighted by the mere fact that her death and burial is recorded. Women here are regarded as co-worshippers in a well-established pattern of worship.

In Numbers 12 she is again presented as one of the three leaders of the people, although Moses is obviously the God-chosen overall leader. Here, Miriam's exemplary life of service to the nation, that began with the rescue of baby brother Moses from an early death in the Nile, is blackened by an act of dissent bordering on rebellion. Numbers 12:1 records her and brother Aaron's attack on Moses: "Miriam and Aaron spoke against Moses because of the Cushite [Ethiopian] woman whom he had married, for he had married a Cushite woman." There also seems to be a significant amount of resentment that has built up in her and brother Aaron as well: "And they said, Has the Lord indeed spoken only

---

8. Bushnell, paragraph 151.

through Moses? Has he not spoken through us also? (Num. 12:2). Those who are the greats also have their moments of failure.

While the circumstances of Moses marrying an Ethiopian woman are not expounded upon here, it seems to have angered Miriam in particular since she is mentioned first, ahead of Aaron, in Numbers 12:1, and the verb for "spoke against" is in the feminine form. While both Miriam and Aaron are censured by God for their lack of respect for Moses, the preeminent prophet, only Miriam is punished by God with a skin disease. Why only her?

Some might say that the failure to punish Aaron and punish only Miriam somehow points to her inferiority in relationship to the male chief priest. However, a stronger case could be made that it was her greater, not lesser, importance to the people as the leading female representative of God to the people that incurred the heavier penalty. That she would be an example of God's judgment on dissension highlights her importance, not her lesser status.

If women are not to take the lead over men in any circumstance, what are we to make of other examples of women called and used by God instead of men? Why did God send Deborah to get Barak motivated to carry out the plan of God? (Judg. 4:6). God used another woman, Manoah's wife, to tell her husband about the announcement of the child she was to bear (Judg. 13:2–7). And if the prophet Jeremiah was already ministering in Jerusalem, why did Hilkiah the priest, along with other dignitaries from the palace, seek out Huldah, the prophetess, about the meaning of the recently discovered Law of Moses (2 Kings 22:14; 2 Chron. 34:22) rather than consulting the prophet Jeremiah? Huldah held nothing back as she declared thrice over, "This is what the Lord, the God of Israel says" (2 Chron. 34:23, 24, 26). Her exposition of a half dozen or more texts from Deuteronomy 29:20, 23, and 25–29 was a thunderous rebuke of the nation of Judah and King Josiah with an apparent anointing from God.

Nor was God displeased with Abigail (1 Sam. 25), who showed more discernment and wisdom than her foolish husband Nabal, who almost led that whole household into mortal danger had not Abigail intervened. Not only did King David praise her for preventing him from acting foolishly, but Scripture attests to the rightness of her actions over against those of her husband Nabal by saying that ten days later, the Lord struck Nabal down so that he died.

It was *not* the Old Testament that placed women in an inferior position, but a set of rabbinic traditions that were later infused with more pagan ideas that introduced these deviant views of women.

5. First Timothy 2:8–15 affirms that women are encouraged to lead in pub-
    lic prayers and to teach, but only after they have been taught.

The apostle Paul, under the direction of the Holy Spirit, says to men in 1
Timothy 2 that "I want men everywhere to lift up holy hands in prayer" (v. 8),
but he warned men to beware of leading outwardly in prayer while inwardly
doing a slow burn over some dispute or hidden anger over some problem with
another person. This was a problem that men needed to handle.

From there Paul went on to draw a strong comparison. He began verse 9
with the Greek word *hosautos*, meaning "in like manner" or "similarly." The
NIV and other versions tend to drop out this expression or to soften this link-
ing word with a rendering that is less emphatic. For example, the NIV says "I
also want, . . ." The apostle wants the women to do something similar to what
he had just instructed the men to do, that is, to pray in public. I say "in public" because it is prayer with a "lifting up of holy hands" or outstretched arms,
as is common when publicly blessing God's people. Thus, the Greek word for
"in like manner" repeats the whole previous sentence's circumstances except
the warning is different: men have trouble in overly internalizing anger and
disputes while trying to pray effectively in public as if nothing was wrong or
troubling them. Women, however, have trouble sometimes realizing that God
meant them to concentrate on inner, spiritual beauty ahead of outer, physical
beauty. Their temptation was to focus on physical beauty and their attractive-
ness to men, so they dressed to the nine, as we might say, in the cultural fash-
ion of their day. The apostle is essentially saying, "Wait—not here, not that
way!" Women must dress modestly while offering prayers in public so not to
call attention to themselves, but to God.

The issue here is not what women might look like when they offered private
prayers in their own homes. Accordingly, the apostle wants women to participate with men in the public service of the church by offering prayers. There can
be no debate over this point, unless someone knows how we can get rid of *hosautos* in this text!

A. J. Gordon, one of the founders of Gordon-Conwell Theological Seminary, quipped (after noting 1 Timothy 2:8–15 and 1 Corinthians 11:5—"Every
woman who prays or prophesies") is sometimes objectionable to some. Gordon
intoned: "It is quite incredible, on the contrary, that the apostle should give
himself the trouble to prune a custom, which he desired to [totally] uproot, or
that he should spend his breath condemning a forbidden method of doing a for-

bidden thing."[9] Exactly so! On the contrary, God wanted women to participate in public services both in prayer and, as we will see, by prophesying; however, they were to be careful of their dress so as not to draw attention to themselves.

In our culture we might unconsciously assume that this call to "modesty" concerns *provocative* clothing and the much more sexualized fashions worn today by women (and even men!). However, in the first century, clothing and women's accouterments were more often used as a way to show off one's wealth. Paul is concerned about the first-century version of "bling." He admonishes them that their "adornment must not be with braided hair and gold or pearls or expensive clothing, but with good deeds, as is proper for women who profess reverence for God" (1 Tim. 2:9–10 ESV).

Similarly, the apostle Peter confronted this same problem in his early letter to the churches when he warned, "Do not let your adorning be external—the braiding of hair and the putting on of gold jewelry, or the clothing you wear—but let your adorning be the hidden person of the heart with the imperishable beauty of a gentle and quiet spirit, which in God's sight is very precious" (1 Peter 3:3–4 ESV). Essentially, Peter is warning the wealthy not to flaunt their riches and rub them in the faces of their poorer brothers and sisters in Christ. The outward display of status symbols means nothing to God.

Now the central point of this passage, one indeed that would have been revolutionary for Paul's day, comes in 1 Timothy 2:11—"Let a woman . . . learn!" This was a real bombshell for that day—why would anyone want to do something like that? The Hebrews did not let their women learn, nor did the Greeks, Romans, or even the pagans. Why should the Christians start such a strange custom since it had never been heard of or done by anyone else before this? But Paul is insistent: it is the only imperative in the passage. It is this verb, *manthaneto,* "let [the women] learn," which would have drawn everyone's attention and potential ire when this text was first written. Unfortunately, we do not have a third person imperative form in English, so our "let [them] learn" sounds as if it is mere permission, but do not mistake the apostle's intention here. He *orders* the believers to teach women the gospel in all its magnificence.

Yes, some respond, a woman should learn, but however she learns, she must do so "in silence," and "in full submission." Some want to argue that this submission is to her husband. On the contrary, the "subjection" is most

---

9. Adoniram Judson Gordon, "The Ministry of Women," *Missionary Review of the World* VII, new series, December 1894.

naturally understood as being *to God*, as shown in the words immediately pro-ceeding in verse 10: "as women who profess reverence for God." Alternatively, it might mean submission to her teacher, as is encouraged in 1 Corinthians 16:16 or Hebrews 13:17. Likewise, it is not total "silence" that is required of the female learner any more than the same "silence" is required of men when they work or eat their lunches (2 Thess. 3:12). In both cases the Greek word *hesuchia* is better rendered as "quietness" or, even better, "a quiet spirit." Thus it is not an absolute silence that is required here of women any more than of men. But even with this instruction on the demeanor and attitudes of the female learner noted here, it would not have been accepted by Jewish teach-ing of that time. The Jewish attitude was clearly the opposite: "Let the law be burned rather than committed to a woman" and "he who teaches his daughter the law, is as though he taught her sin." So taught the rabbis of the first and second centuries AD.[10]

OK, say some objectors, but why is it that Paul goes on to say in 1 Timothy 2:12 that he does "not permit a woman to teach or to have authority over a man"? Had Paul suddenly changed his mind after demanding that women pray in public and prophesy in the body of believers after being taught?

If this is an absolute command allowing no exceptions, then why does Paul instruct women to teach other women in Titus 2:4? Should he not also have silenced Priscilla, whose name usually precedes Aquila's in Greek order of the names in the book of Acts (as in Acts 18:26, despite the fact that some trans-lations put it the other way around—"Aquila and Priscilla"), and who clearly taught as well? And what of poor Timothy, whose father was a Gentile? Paul attributed Timothy's biblical learning and instruction to his mother and grand-mother (2 Tim. 1:5), which seems to be an unauthorized source of instruction for a young man, at least unauthorized according to those who take the view that women teaching men is forbidden by Scripture. Hopefully they taught him, as some would have it, before he was seven years old, as at least one prominent Bible teacher oddly teaches that women should not teach boys once they pass their seventh birthday. Don't ask me why—it is just affirmed as a known truth by a well-known teacher.

So what is the answer?

---

10. So taught Eliezer Ben Hyrcanus, one of the most prominent *Tannaim* or Jewish teachers from approximately AD 10 to 220 whose teachings were often repeated in the Mishnah, the written collection of the oral teachings on the Law that was collected and written down around AD 200.

Yes, women must not teach or exercise authority over a man, but the reasons are found in the context that follows in verses 13 and 14. Here Paul expresses his strong preference and his own desires (though he, too, has the mind of the Lord even in this) for he uses the Greek word *epitrepo*, "I do [not] permit." This form is exactly the same form that Paul used in 1 Corinthians 7:7: "I *wish* that all men were as I am [unmarried]." But he does not use the imperative form of the verb now as he did with directing that women be taught. So why does he not wish or want women "to teach (note there should be no comma here, for the Greek text is without our systems of punctuation) or to control a man."

The reasons cited in the text are these: Adam was "shaped/formed/molded/ fashioned" first. What will throw everything off track here is to view this first reason as an argument from "the orders of creation," i.e., Adam was created first and then came Eve. But if that holds water, what if the animals demanded their rights since they got here even before Adam was created—First is first! However, Paul did not use the Greek word *ktizo,* "to create," in this context; instead, he used *plasso*, which is also found, as it is used here, in descriptions of the "orders of *education.*" It is the same root from which we today get our word for "plastic." It refers in Greek to all sorts of formal thinking, teaching, and instruction in society. Therefore, Paul's restriction or wish that women not teach or exercise authority, however we desire to view it here, is incumbent on women only so long as they remain untaught. Presumably, as soon as the women were taught, they would be allowed to teach, lead in public prayer, and to exercise leadership much as some did in the examples already noted from the Old Testament. Otherwise, how else can we avoid formulating an unnecessary contradiction between Paul's teaching and his practices as taught and permitted elsewhere in Scripture?

Adam had the "jump start" on Eve in education, for God had previously walked and talked with Adam in the Garden of Eden. But that is how Satan, the snake, was able to trick Eve. It appeared as if she had planned to hold her tongue when the tempter spoke to her, but when "the Serpent" subtly suggested that God had set up impossibly narrow rules and then "the Serpent" even went on to deliberately distort what God had said. Eve almost involuntarily sprung to God's defense as well as the couples' own standing before the tempter. In this way she was sucked into the vortex of the Evil One's trickery and deception while she still was untaught in the tricky ways of the Devil.

Why Adam did not intervene, taught as he was, I cannot say. He just left Eve rattle on—the dummy! So what Paul teaches here is this: Adam himself was not "deceived," but Eve was "*thoroughly* deceived" (the Greek text here has the same verb but adds an intensifying preposition attached to the same verb for Eve). The best way to deceive or trick someone is to do so when they have not been taught. It is this Greek verb, *exapatetheisa*, "to thoroughly deceive," that shifts the word *plasso* from the secondary meaning "to form" as in creation, to the primary meaning usually associated with this verb "to shape (socially or educationally)." Thus, there are two reasons why women, according to Paul, should not teach: (1) they have not as yet had a chance to be taught; and (2) they can all too easily be tricked and deceived when they have not yet been taught. Unfortunately, Adam too sinned, but did so being fully cognizant of what was going on. Eve, on the other hand, seemed to be really hoodwinked and attacked, as if by ambush, because she had not as yet had all the advantages of walking and talking more extensively with God in the garden of Eden or of learning as Adam had already experienced.

And then there is the extremely difficult verse, 1 Timothy 2:15, for which some thirty major interpretations exist. But the context is king so the flow of the argument is this: Don't try to put down women just because Eve was really hoodwinked and tricked by Satan. Remember, God chose a woman through whom the promised child came and not a man! So men, be careful and kind in your assessments and in your comments about these women that God has given to us to end our loneliness.

With this understanding of 1 Timothy 2:8–15, we can see now how Paul could also allow women to "pray and prophesy" in 1 Corinthians 11:5 and even be more emphatic in 1 Corinthians 14:31 where "all may prophesy" so that "all may learn" and "all may be encouraged." The same "all" who were learning and being encouraged were the same ones who made up the identity of those who may prophesy—"all." If some wish to cavil over the word "prophesy," it can be noted in 1 Corinthians 14:3 that "Everyone who prophesies speaks to mortals for their strengthening, encouragement and comfort." That sounds like a definition of preaching, doesn't it?

6. In 1 Corinthians 14:34–38, it is the Talmud, not the Old Testament law, which taught that women must be silent and only talk at home.

The New International Version, along with other translations, errs badly by interpretively giving a capital letter to the word "Law" when translating verse 34. The problem simply put is this: Nowhere in the Old Testament does it teach or even imply what is claimed in these words in this context! No law in the Old Testament, much less the Torah, can be cited to teach that a woman "must be in submission" and "remain silent" and if she wants to know or ask about anything, she "should ask [her own] husband at home." Women spoke freely in public in both testaments.

It was in the Jewish synagogues that women were not allowed to speak and usually had to sit in the balcony of the synagogues. Thus, the "law" referred to here is the Jewish Oral Law, the same one Jesus referred to in the Sermon on the Mount. Jesus here corrected the false interpretations of the rabbis—"You have heard it said"—which he contrasted with the written word of Scripture and its true intention. Yes, some Jewish rabbis taught that "Out of respect to the congregation, a woman should not herself read the law." Also, "It is a shame for a woman to let her voice be heard among men." Even in our own times, this view is still held by some Orthodox Jews in Israel: "Rabbi Shlomo Aviner, another prominent spiritual leader of the Zionist-religious public, ruled that girls were absolutely forbidden from studying Gemara (Rabbinic commentary) because this was 'unfitting for their souls.'"[11]

One scholar has singled out this interpretation of this passage as an example of a hermeneutical "fallacy" in interpretation. We ask this scholar then to point to the place in God's "Law" where any of these concepts are taught or even alluded to in order to support his labeling of this view as an "exegetical fallacy." Failing that, the text calls for a repudiation of all alternative views that in some way or another demand that these teachings are ordained and prescribed by God.

If Paul is not quoting from Scripture but rather from a letter of inquiry that was sent to him by the Corinthians, asking if they too should observe such rules of quietude for women in the church (which used rabbinic teaching as its norm), can we show any other places where the same type of quoting from external sources is used by Paul as a basis for a following rebuttal in the same book? Yes, in 1 Corinthians 6:12; 8:8: and 10:23, Paul quotes from an outside aphorism, "All things are lawful for me." But Paul immediately refutes such a statement as he does in 1 Corinthians 14:36. Paul shouts, "What?" "Did the word of God originate with you? Or are you the only ones [masculine plural] it has reached?" To paraphrase: "Fiddlesticks," objects Paul. "You can't really be serious, can you? That you guys are the *only* ones able to get the meaning of the word of God?"

11. Kobi Nahshoni, "Rabbi Eliyahu: Women Shouldn't Study Gemara," *Jewish World*, NetNews.com, http://www.ynetnews.com/articles/0,7340,L-3412203,00.html (accessed March 14, 2015).

If that is so, what was Pentecost all about? Did we not see the immediate "now" of Old Testament prophecy being fulfilled (even if it was not *all* of the future events predicted in this prophecy of Joel 2:28–29)? The Holy Spirit would be poured out on all, regardless of their age, *gender*, or their race? The Holy Spirit came upon women as well as men—the text says so! And what shall we say about Psalm 68:11? There Scripture proclaims, "The Lord announced the word, and great was the company [women preachers] of those who proclaimed it." The word for "company" is a feminine plural form. Note the way that some translations bring out the sense of this text:

> NASB—The Lord gives the command; The women who proclaim the good tidings are a great host.

> ESV—The Lord gives the word; the women who announce the news are a great host.

> HCSB—The Lord gave the command; a great company of women brought the good news.

> NET—The Lord speaks; many, many women spread the good news.

> RV—The Lord giveth the word: the women that publish the tidings are a great host

Here the good news spoken by God, perhaps a royal decree or the news that the enemies of God's people have run in terror (v. 12), is spread by a large group of female heralds. As someone has said, the easiest way to detect that you are dealing with a dead horse is if you prop it up on one end, and then the other end falls down! That is what so many are doing in their interpretations of these texts.

7. In 1 Corinthians 11:2–16 women are to exercise authority and veils are not required

We have already noted the Old Testament background for the women to have strength, power, or authority invested in themselves in Genesis 2:18. That is, no doubt what Paul was alluding to in 1 Corinthians 11:10. We also noted how false and thoroughly intrusive was the thought that a "veil as a sign of authority" was forced into the translations of this verse from the days of the Gnostic religions, both in Paul's day and in the subsequent times. Paul would certainly never have stood for such impositions on the Word of God that stands written for all time and eternity—nor should we. Away with all impositions of a "veil" or veiled references!

At the heart of this passage in 1 Corinthians 11:1–16 is Paul's desire to stop the practice that had come over from the synagogue, in which men veiled their heads in the worship service. The head covering that was used was called a *tallith*, worn by all men during the morning prayers and on Sabbath days and Holy Days. This *tallith* was also worn by the *hazzan* (the leader of worship) whenever he prayed in front of the ark in the synagogue that held Scripture texts and by the one who was called up to read the scroll of the law at the "reading desk" (the *almemar*). Remarkable as well is the fact that the Romans were also veiled when they worshipped, so both the Jewish and Roman converts would have been accustomed to such veiling practices as part of the liturgy of the worship service.

From the Jewish perspective, Paul was anxious to make clear that such a veiling of the *tallith* was not only a sign of reverence to God, but unfortunately it was also a sign of condemnation for sin and of guilt of its wearer before the Almighty. But how could such signs be worn when "there is therefore now no condemnation to those who are in Christ Jesus" (Rom. 12:1)?

Paul, therefore, forbids men to be veiled. He permits a woman to be veiled, but it is only by permission, not by obligation that he does so. His real preference is for women to likewise be unveiled before God, men, and angels, especially when women are addressing God in prayer. On the contrary, women should not feel embarrassed about having their heads uncovered, for their hair is given to them as their "glory." In fact, the church has no prescribed rule or custom about needing a veil. Here again some translations said the exact opposite by noting that the church had "no other" rule than custom required; but the Greek will not allow such an infelicity, for the Greek reads that the church had "no such" rule.

Men and women are not independent of one another (1 Cor. 11:1–12) for God made woman "from the man," while God now brings all men "through the woman." Regardless, "all things are of God," so neither gender gets bragging rights or one-upmanship here.

Conclusion

God and the Scriptures are far from being repressive, hostile, or demeaning to women; instead, God and the Scriptures constantly elevate women and give them places of honor and credit along with their male counterparts. Both males and females are equal in being given a head covering of hair. In 1 Corinthians 11:15, the woman is given her hair *anti*, "in place of" or "instead of," a hat or covering. And if anyone wishes to get testy over the whole matter of requiring women to wear some kind of covering, as we have already noted, then Paul says in 1 Corinthians 11:16, "we have no such practice" that requires women to wear a covering. Note even here how the translations reverse the whole meaning of the Greek text and say, as the NIV says, "We have *no other* practice" (emphasis mine), which infers this is the only one and that is that women must wear a covering when they worship. How difficult it is to reverse some habits and traditions, much less some translations!

Together men and women are "joint heirs of the grace of life" (1 Peter 3:7, 11) submitting themselves to the Lord and to each other (Eph. 5:21). Each owes to the other love, respect, and an appreciation for the sphere of authority given to each one as part of the gifts of the Spirit. These gifts are never gender-coded in Scripture, but they are meant for the blessing of the whole body of Christ.

May Christ's church take the lead in setting forth a whole new standard for the giftedness and ministry of women, even against the conflicting assertions of male prominence and leadership on the one hand and radical feminist independence on the other. Neither of these extremes reflects the intent and purposes of Scripture for men and women. *Sola Scriptura* must be the rallying point once again as it has been time after time in history. May Christ's church find the rest, comfort and admonition of Scripture on the teaching of women and their ministries to be in God's final word for our day as it has been in the past.

Discussion Questions

1. What is the best translation for the word "Helper" in Genesis 2:18 according to the chapter you read in this book? How does this translation help us to understand what the apostle Paul said rested on the head of a woman in 1 Corinthians 11:10?

2. Is Genesis 3:16 a command that men "must rule" over wives? Is this passage a blessing passage or a curse passage in Genesis? If the word "must rule" is an incorrect rendering of the verb, how then shall we interpret Genesis 4:7 which seems to have the same construction?

3. According to Genesis 3:16, do women have natural sexual desires or lusts for men as a result of the Fall? If not, how did such ideas get into the text of Scripture?

4. In 1 Timothy 2:8–15, are women encouraged or discouraged from leading in public prayer and teaching others? What was the absolute command of this passage in 1 Timothy 2:11? Why does the English translation not sound like an imperative at all?

5. How was Adam "shaped, formed" first before Eve according to 1 Timothy 2? Does this imply that in the "orders of creation," the man is to take the lead?

6. Where were women taught that they must be silent and only ask their husbands at home if they have a question?

7. Does the church have a rule that women must wear a veil in church, according to 1 Corinthians 11:2–16?

10

The God of Freedom with Food or the God of Forbidden Food?

Question: *Does God still maintain distinctions of clean and unclean foods or has God declared all foods clean?*

If all Scripture is inspired by God and it all is useful for various purposes (as 2 Tim. 3:15–16 tells us), then what are we to think about the distinctions between clean and unclean animals recorded in Leviticus 11 and Deuteronomy 14:3–20? These laws, as much as anything else, seem to corroborate the fact that the Old Testament is different from the New Testament and that God has adopted a different stance on the matter of foods. For contemporary Christians, these laws seem to be some strange laws indeed—ones that for this day, at the very least, are (or seem to be) antiquated!

Notions about "ritual purity" and "impurity," as well as "clean" and "unclean" are both difficult to explain and to understand. As moderns, we have little experience living in a distinct community and culture defined by practices of ritual and worship. In their original setting, these concepts were related to a person's fitness or qualification to enter the worship of God in the tabernacle or temple. Moreover, the words seem to imply something about general hygiene, but this is not true in most cases. The issues were not a matter of hygiene or sanitation; instead, these rules must be understood as belonging in large measure to matters related purely to ritual states of worshippers. How one could interact and participate fully in community life was determined by ones adherence to specific regulations that defined an acceptable ritual state. It is worth noting that the first ten chapters of Leviticus focuses on matters related to worship.

The Old Testament regulations regarding clean/unclean conditions addressed a variety of issues that were commonly experienced by the children of Israel. For example:

- contact with a dead animal (Lev. 11)
- childbirth (Lev. 12)
- various kinds of skin diseases (Lev. 13–14)
- bodily fluids (Lev. 15)
- menstruation (Lev. 15)

Interestingly, all of these, in one very real sense, were "normal" conditions of daily living in that time of history where extended families and tribal groups lived in close proximity. The "daily" quality of these issues could be a clue as to the reason for distinctions between clean and unclean. They should not be confused with moral or ethical conditions. The farmer who encountered a dead goat in his field did not commit "sin" by burying it. He just couldn't participate in ritual activities in the community until the prescribed ritual of cleansing was performed. The number of issues addressed by matters clean and unclean did serve as a reminder (daily) that just as God could only be served and worshipped by the ritually clean, so too He could only be truly worshipped by the moral and spiritual clean of heart. As God Himself was holy, they too had been called to holy.

A second benefit of the cleanliness code was that it also reminded the children of Israel that they had been set apart by God. By living differently, they were daily reminded that they were to *be* different: "I am the Lord your God. You shall not do as they do in the land of Egypt where you lived, and you shall not do as they do in the land of Canaan, to which I am bringing you" (Lev. 18:3 ESV). Therefore, any emulation of the pagan religions and practices of the people surrounding them were to be shunned and forsaken.

One of the most prominent areas covered in the regulations of Leviticus are rules concerning food: categories of clean and unclean. It is a distinction that continues today in the Jewish practice of "keeping kosher" (based on the Hebrew word *kashut*, meaning "fit" or "proper"). While the present-day practice of kosher eating involves factors such as how meat is slaughtered and what utensils are used in preparation, at its heart are the Levitical categories of clean and unclean. The category of "clean" animals meant that there were animals that could be eaten by the Israelites.

The unclean ones were forbidden to be used as food for those called to be God's holy people. This seems simple enough but also raises a further question: Why were some animals pronounced unclean while others were declared to be clean?

This subject seems strange to modern people living in developed economies where we have become accustomed to thinking about religion as something that affects only the spirit and is completely independent of bodily and external conditions. But it must be remembered that our Lord Jesus repeatedly referred to the book of Leviticus as the Word of God. Therefore, before we dismiss the idea of clean and unclean, we should pay attention to the message and claims of Leviticus 11 to see if it has any modern relevance to us.[1]

Leviticus 11 is almost evenly divided into two sections: Verses 1–23 treat the law of clean and unclean, and verses 24–40 treat defilement by virtue of contact with dead bodies. The chapter ends with a final appeal and a summary in verses 41–47. The structure of this chapter falls into six divisions clearly demarcated by the words "this," or "these" (verses 2, 9, 13, 24, 29, and 46). Regulations concerning clean and unclean land animals are found in verses 1–8; clean and unclean aquatic creatures in verses 9–12; clean and unclean flying creatures in verses 13–23; pollution from land animals in verses 24–28; pollution from swarming creatures in verses 29–45; and a summary concludes the chapter in verses 46–47.

Determining the principles by which certain animals were permitted to be eaten and others were forbidden to be consumed is the more difficult question. We are told in verses 43–45 that Israel was to abstain from eating or touching anything that was unclean on the grounds that she was holy, just as the Lord their God was holy. But this only increases our inquisitiveness. What possible connection can there be between eating or abstaining from eating animals that do or do not chew the cud, or fish that have or do not have scales, and the personal holiness of an individual Israelite?

Various Explanations for Distinguishing Between Clean and Unclean

A Mystical Connection. Some have supposed that there is a mystical connection between the soul and the body, such that the soul can be defiled by the food

---

1. For further discussion, see Walter C. Kaiser, Jr., "The Book of Leviticus: Introduction, Commentary and Reflections," in *The New Interpreter's Bible,* ed. Leander E. Keck (Nashville: Abingdon Press, 1994), 1:985–1191, especially 1074–1083.

the body receives. The evidence for this, however, is slight. In the Greek Sep-
tuagint translation, Leviticus 11:44 is rendered "you shall not defile your souls."
But the Hebrew word for "souls" (*nephesh*) as used here is an equivalent for the
English "yourselves," as it is properly rendered in both the Authorized Version
(KJV) and the Revised Version. The rendering "yourselves" is to be preferred
here. So there is no evidence for a mystical soul-body connection regarding food.

A Way of Keeping Israel Separate from the Nations. This explanation argues
that God wanted to keep Israel separate from the other nations, so he gave them
a special dietetic code in order to distinguish them and set them apart from others who observed them from the outside. These laws, however, seemed to be already existing (20:24–25). And at any rate, this would not explain the principle
by which some animals were considered clean while others were not.

A Divine Moral Discipline in Self-Restraint and Control. This view holds
that the Lord was trying to build types of moral restraint and discipline by giving these rules. While these rules did impose certain limitations on Israel, and
therefore restrictions in their approach to God, this does not explain why these
restrictions should be of one kind and not another. So this explanation is likewise not completely satisfying.

Some Animals Are Unhygienic. The medieval Jewish philosopher and rabbinic scholar Maimonides (1135?–1204) was one of the most prominent
historical figures to teach that eating some animals was detrimental to people's health. Some modern commentaries on Leviticus use this argument
from Maimonides extensively since it is true that pigs can contain certain
harmful bacteria or parasites, especially so in the ancient world. But as true
as this may be, the Bible never gives this as a reason for the prohibition.

This medieval view has been expanded in the current "scientific view" that
holds that the distinctions between clean and unclean reflect actual biological and physiological differences between the animals and that the benefits of
eating "clean" animals can be scientifically proven. Herbivores are said to have
digestive systems that "cleanse" their food, as do fowls that have a craw and
gizzard. Omnivores, such as pigs, not only eat detestable food such as garbage,
but also lack a more complex digestive system to filter out pathogens and toxins. Shellfish, which are scavengers, also take in decayed matter and are carriers
of disease and toxins.

While this view has some appeal at the surface level, its basis in science is rather thin. The digestive systems of the "clean" animals are not systems for "cleansing" their food and thus the nutrients passed onto their muscles. Many birds, both clean and unclean, have similar digestive systems. If the distinctions between clean and unclean were based in science, then the reasons for those distinctions were unknown for thousands of years.

It Is an Allegory. This very old explanation sees animals as symbols either for good or evil. Thus, animals that chew the cud are clean, which means (according to this interpretation) that human beings should "chew" or "meditate" on the Law of God. This explanation was first given in the Letter of Aristeas (second-century BC), which states that "the parting of the hoof and the dividing of the claws symbolize discrimination in our every action with a view to what is right."[2] Similarly, the author of the Epistle of Barnabas, one of the Apostolic church fathers, frequently allegorized the Scriptures and claimed that the animals in these texts were not literal animals at all—these rules applied only to spiritual things. These "animals" are really people with whom the faithful should or should not mix. This view continued to be popular all the way up to the nineteenth century when the dispensationalist Plymouth Brethren writer C. H. M. (Charles H. Mackintosh) argued for the same symbolic and allegorical meanings. This interpretation, however, is also most unlikely.

Integrity and the "Normal." More recently, biblical scholars have focused more on the issue of "completeness" in Leviticus 11. Things that were not whole were declared to be "unclean" as they lacked integrity and completeness. What was "normal" for an animal belonged to the essence of that animal. This aligned with the accepted "norm" for an animal, as understood by the Israelites, whose living depended on domesticate animals such as goats, sheep, cows, and various fowls. It was "normal" for a land animal to have certain kind of hooves for running, for fish to have fins for swimming, and for birds to have wings for flying. Those who lacked one or more of these "normal" features in their category were not whole and therefore were unclean. Other factors such as cud chewing or food

---

2. The *Letter of Aristeas* purports to relate the history of the translation of the Hebrew Bible into Greek by seventy-two scholars sent from Jerusalem to Egypt at the request of the Egyptian king Ptolemy II Philadelphus in the third century BC. Most scholars conclude that it is a later work of fiction, designed to support the superiority of Judaism and the Hebrew Bible against pagan detractors.

source (in the case of carrion eaters) was taken into account. This view has been widely put forth by Mary Douglas.[3] For Douglas the notion of "wholeness" or "normativity" was key to determining distinctions in the animal realm. But her concepts of "normativity" run counter to the creation account where all things were declared "good" as they came from the hand of God.

Wholeness and Holiness. God made life to be whole and complete. Accordingly, knowing what was clean or unclean was a matter of knowing about the wholeness of life, its integrity and completeness. All of this reflected the "holiness of God," which is the focus of Leviticus 20:25–26:

> You must therefore make a distinction between clean and un-
> clean animals and between unclean and clean birds. Do not
> defile yourselves by any animal or bird or anything that moves
> along the ground—those which I have set apart as unclean for
> you. You are to be holy to me because I, the LORD, am holy,
> and I have set you apart from the nations to be my own.

Wholeness is the opposite of being "mixed" in our commitment to the Lord. Holiness means "being completely set apart to God." A life of godliness, then, is an imitation of God. It is a holiness that has to do with the body as much as with the soul, even down to the mundane matters of our eating and drinking. As such, the body is the instrument and organ of the soul. The body and the physical are just as important as the soul and the spiritual part of a being! Thus, the clean/unclean distinctions served as a self-evident reminder that the spiritual cannot and must not be divorced from the material. Every time an Israelite ate food or had to follow the prescribe ritual for cleansing, it was a reminder that the physical, the spiritual, the ritual, and the moral were all bound together.

While this view does not answer every question we may have as to why God chose specific animals for a specific category, it does provide us with a conceptual framework that explains the reason for and the benefit of the distinctions.

We are still left, then, with a question to address: What is the significance or application of the regulations regarding clean and unclean for believers today? Were these regulations dispensed with at the coming of Jesus the Messiah? Let's

---

3.   Mary Douglas, *Implicit Meanings: Essays in Anthropology* (Boston: Routledge & Kegan, 1975), 266.

look at several passages that are cited as evidence in support of the idea that these concepts are no longer relevant or have any value.

Did Jesus Declare All Foods Clean?

It has often been said, in Mark 7:19, "Jesus declared all foods clean." If that is so, who is to say that eating pork, camel, or llama, or anything else for that matter, is unclean or possibly anti-Scriptural?

But there is a major problem with this teaching, or at least this particular rendering of Mark 7:19: The Greek manuscripts of Mark 7:19 do not actually contain the words "Jesus declared." Note how the NIV rendered this text:

> Again, Jesus called the crowd to him and said, "Listen to me, everyone, and understand this. Nothing outside a man can make him 'unclean' by going into him. Rather, it is what comes out of a man that makes him 'unclean.' If anyone has ears to hear, let him hear."
>
> After he had left the crowd and entered the house, his disciples asked him about this parable. "Are you so dull?" he asked. "Don't you see that nothing that enters a man from the outside can make him 'unclean'? For it doesn't go into his heart but into his stomach, and then out of his body." In saying this, Jesus declared all foods "clean." [The ESV rendering is similar].

At issue in translating this verse is a textual problem. Most manuscripts (but not the earliest or most authoritative) have the Greek word for "purging" or "cleansing"—a Greek participle—as a neuter participle. Some important Greek manuscripts, however, have this participle in the masculine form. This raises a textual issue and an interpretive issue.

The textual issue involves deciding which reading should be followed—the one found in most Greek manuscripts of Mark or the one found in some manuscripts seen as having more authority? How can the difference in the form of one letter (that changes the participle from a neuter to a masculine form) be explained? Is there a reason one form would have been changed to the other? Either side of this question can make a case for their preferred reading.

If the masculine participle is the correct reading, many translators see the referent as the subject of the sentence found in verse 18—"*he* said." Therefore, the participle is attributed to Jesus, and the translator clarifies the grammar by inserting the words "he said."

If the neuter participle is the correct reading, the closest referent is the Greek word for "toilet" or "sewer"—"For it does not enter his heart but his stomach, and then goes out into the *sewer*" (NET). So the participle is further explaining the preceding action.

But let us first look at the context of Mark 7:14–19. The Sanhedrin had heard enough reports about Jesus that it was time to investigate to determine if he truly was from God or not. When the investigative delegation arrived in the region of Galilee, they immediately found that Jesus and his disciples had failed to wash their hands before eating (7:1–5), which contradicted one of their time-honored rules. This command did not originate, of course, in the Torah, but it was a part of the Jewish oral tradition; in fact a whole section of the Mishnah (the written collection of the Jewish oral law) was dedicated to the matter of washing one's hands.

When they asked Jesus why his disciples did not live according to the tradition of the Jewish people (7:5), Jesus responded with a quote from Isaiah 29:13, where people honored the Lord with their lips, but their hearts were far from him. Instead, Jesus observed, they pay more attention to the rules of ordinary mortals than to the real rules of God found in the Torah. They had a habit of observing their own traditions rather than the word of God (7:9–13).

Jesus went on to announce to the crowd that it is not what goes into a man that makes him unclean (such as eating food with unwashed hands), but what comes out. When they had gone into the house, the disciples said in effect, "We don't get it!" Jesus had to explain that ritual purity was not the issue he was addressing; it was instead the matter of the uncleanness of the heart. Food is not able to enter into a person's heart; it goes into his stomach and then empties into the latrine, thereby purging or cleansing the food used by the body.

Some correctly understand that the words "Thus he declared" or "in saying this," were not part of the Greek text, but that the translator added them to the text to give what he though was the sense of the passage. However, the Greek literally just says: "purging all foods." Rather than talking about what foods were clean or unclean, Jesus was talking about bodily elimination.

Therefore, this text in Mark 7:19 cannot be used to say Jesus reversed the teaching of the Pentateuch by "making all foods clean." The text simply does not say that! Moreover, how could Jesus take such a position in a context that accuses these Jewish leaders of the very thing he would thereby be doing? This text did not apply to that question.

Did Peter's Vision in Acts 10 Make All Animals Clean?

If Mark 7 is not relevant to our question of what is clean or unclean, what about Acts 10? The narrative in Acts 10 relates how Peter was staying at the house of Simon the Tanner in Joppa. Peter had gone up on the roof of that house to pray, but as he prayed he had a vision. In his vision, he saw a sheet repeatedly let down from heaven with clean and unclean animals in it (10:13). Then he heard a voice say, "Get up, Peter, kill and eat!" Surely, that must have been a sign from heaven that what previously had been thought to be out of bounds as unclean food was now changed and was approved by God as a new food source—or at least that was possibly the initial thought that must have come to the minds of some as they heard about this vision.

But Peter's own interpretation of the vision did not focus in on the fact that "all foods are clean;" instead, as he explained it in Acts 10:28, "God had shown [him] that I should call no man common or unclean." Therefore, the sheet that had been let down three times with its invitation to "kill and eat" was understood *metaphorically* to be speaking of clean and supposed unclean human beings, and not about clean or unclean foods. That is, no one should designate any one group of humans as being unclean or ritually impure or as being ethnically undesirable. God wanted Peter to go with the men Cornelius had sent to him in order to tell them about the gospel, even though they were just Gentiles. What Peter had regarded up to that point as unclean and unworthy subjects for the gospel, that is, the Gentiles, was not the view God wished Peter to hold. They, too, should hear and believe the good news about Yeshua.

First-century Judaism's oral tradition had loads of rules that prevented Jewish people from entering into the homes of Gentiles or of eating with them. We learn this from John 18:28, Acts 10:28, and Galatians 2:11, 15, as well as from the Jewish Mishnah. But there were no such restrictions in the Torah of Moses—nor, for that matter, anywhere else in the Bible. Note also, even though Peter was urged to "kill and eat," he steadfastly refused saying, "By no means, Lord, for I have never eaten anything unholy and unclean" (10:14). Apparently his response was the correct response to the vision itself in its literal understanding; but God wanted him to get another issue straight—he would now be invited to preach to the Gentiles!

Peter, however, did not get the meaning of this vision immediately, for it perplexed him for some time as he remained there on the roof of Simon the tanner's house. But as he was sifting this all through his mind, the men sent by the Roman centurion, Cornelius, kept calling him. Then it was that the Spirit of God helped Peter, for he explained, "Behold three men are looking for you. But "get up, go downstairs and accompany them without misgivings, for I have sent them myself" (10:19, 20). The vision was all about non-Jewish inquirers who needed to know the Lord, not about the propriety of eating shellfish and pork! It was about entering the houses of Gentiles and sharing with them the good news of the gospel. So Peter went and God blessed his ministry.

What Did Paul Mean by "Nothing Is Unclean in Itself"?

In addition to all of this, had not Paul taught In Romans 14:14 the following? "As one who is in the Lord Jesus, I am fully convinced that no food is unclean in itself. But if anyone regards something as unclean, then for him it is unclean."

This seems to speak to our issue of what was clean versus what was unclean, doesn't it? Is Paul contending that it is all in a person's mind; that is, if you think something is unclean, then for you that is what it is? But Paul did not have the topic of clean and unclean animals or foods in mind when he announced this principle. First-century believers understood that any food or drink that had been offered to an idol was out of bounds for a Christian. Already in Exodus 34:15 Moses had made it clear that such partaking of food offered to idols was in effect like making of a covenant with the idol/god when a person participated in such rituals.

However, the apostle Paul did not have the distinction of clean and unclean in mind when he gave this rule in Romans 14:14. He used the Greek word for "common" in this passage. The word "common" can refer to anything made unfit by contact with idolatry or the like; but the word "unclean" would usually refer to meat such as pork and to the category of foods that were off-limits.

Prime cuts of meat, in that first-century marketplace, had often been first offered as part of a sacrifice to the idols that very morning, or they were left over from the feast to that god or goddess the night before. Paul did not think believers should be overly concerned, seeing how difficult it was to get a cut of meat that had not been involved in worship to an idol in that marketplace. Therefore, he urged believers to eat the meat they could find in the market without asking any questions about its source for conscience sake, for the earth is the Lord's (1 Cor. 10:25–26, quoting Ps. 24:1). Only when the source was known to be from an idol, or where the conscience of another person was involved, one should refuse this meat. Food was rendered "common" by virtue of its contact with Gentiles and/or idolatry. The renderings of this Greek word *koinos,* "common," in the English translations of this text are done as if the word were *akathartos,* "unclean." This is what has caused the problem in this text. Once that is straightened out, the problem disappears.

What About the Four Minimal Requirements of Acts 15?

In the first century there was a major disagreement between the Jewish believers in Jesus as the Messiah with the Gentile believers who were in the church at Antioch in Asia Minor (present-day Turkey). The debate was over whether or not the Gentiles had to be circumcised (perhaps as a test question for the whole matter of keeping kosher)? In effect, the question seemed to be much larger than the issue of circumcision; it was this: must the Gentiles become Jewish in all aspects, as defined under the ritual laws of that day, in order to be saved or at least to have fellowship with the Jewish believers? If the answer was "Yes," then it meant that God did not have the power to save non-Jews unless they became Jews. Salvation, then, would be attached to law-keeping! This became a major battleground.

James, the Jewish titular head of all the believers at that point, came up with four minimal requirements for the Gentile believers. These laws were never meant to be grounds for being converted, but they would help the socialization of the Gentiles into the fellowship of the Jewish community. These were his suggestions, which the Jewish and Gentile believers adopted:

1. They were to abstain from meat offered to idols.

2. They were to abstain from eating blood.

3. They were to abstain from sexual immorality.

4. They were to abstain from meat from strangled animals (Acts 15:20).

These four laws ensured that Gentiles would never take part in the idolatry of the local temples of idolatry and therefore would be conscious of being holy to the Lord. In this manner they could participate in the worship at the Messianic synagogues. While James did not excuse Gentiles from observing the food laws given by Moses by explicit wording, he merely reminded these Gentiles that Moses has been read in synagogues every Sabbath from ancient times until that very day (Acts 15:21). So, as Gentiles participated in those services, they were to pay attention to what they heard as all of God's word was taught—not to mention, of course, their obligation to the Ten Commandments as well. Thus, what this Jerusalem Council accomplished was this: Here were four general rules to get things started. It will satisfy for the moment the questions of the Jewish Messianic crowd and allow them to welcome Gentile believers into the fellowship of their Messianic synagogues. As for the rest of any requirement, let's give the Gentiles time to grow up, James seemed to be saying, for don't forget that Moses is read every week in our services where they too are worshiping with us. James must have assumed that the Spirit of God would do the rest of the work.

Are the Torah's Dietary Laws Labeled by Paul as a "Doctrine of Demons"?

When Paul wrote to Timothy in 1 Timothy 4:1–5, he mentioned a "doctrine of demons," along with "men who forbid marriage and advocate abstaining from foods, which God has created to be gratefully shared in by those who believe and know the truth."

But would it not be blasphemous for Paul to refer to the Torah given by God, if that is what these words "doctrine of demons" means, especially in reference to Leviticus 11 teaching on clean and unclean foods? Note however, especially since there is no prohibition on marriage in the Torah, the claim that this comes from Moses was incorrect from the very start. Instead, Genesis taught married couples were to be fruitful and to multiply.

However, it is clear that early Gnosticism did teach abstinence from marriage, sex, along with abstaining from certain foods. These Gnostics were more influenced by Greek philosophy than they were by the Bible, for they held that the physical world was intrinsically evil and the human body a prison for the spirit of man. Humans being must, they urged, be set free from the physical world so they could soar with the Spirit. They were called "Gnostics" because they alleged that they had a secret knowledge (Greek: *gnosis*) that came by revelation, which of course was not true.

Paul attacked this heresy full bore in Colossians 2:18–23. Who were these persons, he demanded, who wanted to defraud believers by forms of self-abasement, worship of angels, and who insisted on "do not handle, do not taste, do not touch?" But these "elementary principles of the world" were merely the commands and teachings of mortals, who were all destined to perish with use." This was a man-made, self-taught religion; these were not the teachings of the revelation of God in the Torah.

Conclusion

The food laws were and continue to be instructions from God to help both Jewish and Gentile believers to a new sense of wholeness and completeness. Those texts in the New Testament that seem to eliminate these laws are seen to violate their own meaning when judged by the contexts of each citation. God wants his people to be fit and ready to live holy lives to the honor and glory of his name.

Therefore, it is worthwhile to consider how that, as they provided the children of Israel with a daily, visible, and physical reminder of what wholeness and holiness meant, they still have value for believers today. Are we mixed in our devotion to the Lord? Do we minimize and devalue the physical and maintain that it is really only the "spiritual" things of life that matter, thinking that God isn't concerned with our bodies, our diets, or our health? Do we fail to set limits on food, so that we endanger our health, failing to see it as a gift from God to treated with thankfulness, respect, and discipline?

These laws from Leviticus have nothing to do with the personal salvation of any Jew or Gentile nor are they an external means of achieving holiness. However, they do show us that *how* we live is just as important as what we *say* we believe. Those who claim to know and follow Jesus, God's chosen Messiah, are also called to be holy, just as God is holy.

Discussion Questions:

1. What were some of the alleged explanations for distinguishing between the clean and the unclean found in Leviticus 11? What is your estimate of the explanation of "wholeness" as the meaning of this text?

2. Did Jesus declare "all foods clean" in Mark 7:19? What exactly was Jesus' argument in that passage?

3. Did Peter's vision in Acts 20 make all animals clean? What did his vision mean?

4. What did the apostle Paul mean in Romans 14:14 when he said, "No food is unclean in itself"? How should we apply this teaching in our day?

5. What were the four requirements placed on the Gentiles in Acts 15? How should they be understood today?

6. Did Paul's reference to the "doctrine of demons" refer to the five books of Moses in 1 Timothy 4:1–5? To what did it refer?

Bibliography

General Theme

Achtemeier, Elizabeth. *Preaching Hard Texts of the Old Testament*. Peabody, MA: Hendrickson, 1998.

Barton, John. "Marcion Revisited," in *The Canon Debate: On the Origins and Formation of the Bible*. Eds. Lee Martin McDonald and James A. Sanders Peabody, MA: Hendrickson, 2002, 341–54.

Bright, John, *The Authority of the Bible*. Nashville: Abingdon, 1967.

Bultmann, Rudolf, "The Significance of the Old Testament for Christian Faith," in *The Old Testament and Christian Faith*. Ed. Bernhard W. Anderson. New York: Harper & Row, 1963, 8–35.

Collins, John J. "The Zeal of Phinehas: The Bible and the Legitimation of Violence," *Journal of Biblical Literature* 122 (2003): 3–21.

Carroll, R. M. Daniel. *Introduction to the Theory and Practice of Old Testament Ethics*. Grand Rapids: Baker Academic, 2008.

Copan, Paul. *Is God a Moral Monster? Making Sense of the Old Testament God*. Grand Rapids: Baker, 2011.

Davies, Eryl, "The Morally Dubious Passages of the Hebrew Bible: An Examination of Some Proposed Solutions," *Currents in Biblical Research* 3 (2005): 197–228.

Edelman, Diana, "Saul's Battle against Amaleq (1 Sam. 15)," *Journal for the Study of the Old Testament* 35 (1986): 71–84.

Fosdick, Harry Emerson. *A Guide to Understanding the Bible: The Development of Ideas within the Old and New Testaments.* 12th ed. New York: Harper and Brothers, 1938.

Fretheim, Terence E. "God and Violence in the Old Testament," *Word and World* 24 (2004): 18–28.

_____. "I Was Only a Little Angry: Divine Violence in the Prophets," *Interpretation* 58 (2004): 365–75.

Goldingay, John. *Key Questions about Christian Faith: Old Testament Answers.* Grand Rapids: Baker, 2010.

_____. *Key Questions about Biblical Interpretation.* Grand Rapids: Baker, 2011.

Hendel, Ronald S. "When God Acts Immorally," *Bible Review* 7 (1991): 34, 37, 46, 48, 50.

Kaiser, Walter C. Jr., et al., *Hard Sayings of the Bible.* Downers Grove, IL: InterVarsity, 1996.

_____. *The Old Testament Documents: Are They Reliable and Relevant?* Downers Grove, IL: InterVarsity, 2001.

_____. *Recovering the Unity of the Bible: One Continuous Story, Plan, and Purpose.* Chapter 7, "The God of the Old Testament and the New," and chapter 8, "The Morally Offensive Character and Acts of Old Testament Men and Women." Grand Rapids: Zondervan, 2009, 85–110.

Kitchen, Kenneth A. *On the Reliability of the Old Testament.* Grand Rapids: Eerdmans, 2003.

Lamb, David T. *God Behaving Badly: Is the God of the Old Testament Angry, Sexist and Racist?* Downers Grove, IL: InterVarsity, 2011.

Longman, Tremper III. *Making Sense of the Old Testament: Three Crucial Questions.* Grand Rapids: Baker, 1998.

Marshall, I. Howard, "New Testament Perspectives on War," *Evangelical Quarterly* 57 (1985):115–32.

Schlimm, Matthew Richard. *This Strange and Sacred Scripture: Wrestling with the Old Testament Oddities.* Grand Rapids: Baker Academic, 2015.

Seibert, Eric A. *Disturbing Divine Behavior: Troubling Old Testament Images of God.* Minneapolis: Fortress Press, 2009.

Thompson, Alden. *Who's Afraid of the Old Testament God?* Grand Rapids: Zondervan, 1989.

Westermann, Claus. *What Does the Old Testament Say about God?* Ed. Friedemann W. Golka. Atlanta: John Knox, 1979.

Whybray, R. N. "The Immorality of God: Reflections on Some Passages in Genesis, Job, Exodus and Numbers," *Journal for the Study of the Old Testament.* 72 (1996): 89–120.

Wright, Christopher J. H. *The God I Don't Understand.* Grand Rapids: Zondervan, 2008.

Omniscience of God

Fretheim, Terence E. "God and World: Foreknowledge," in *The Suffering of God: An Old Testament Perspective.* Philadelphia, PA: Fortress Press, 1984, 45–59.

_____. *God and World in the Old Testament: A Relational Theology of Creation.* Nashville: Abingdon, 2005.

Helm, Paul. "An Augustinian-Calvinist Response [to the Open Theism view]," in *Four Views*. Eds. James K. Belby and Paul R. Eddy. Downers Grove, IL: InterVarsity, 2001, 61–64.

Pinnock, Clark, et al., *The Openness of God*. Downers Grove, IL: InterVarsity Press, 1994.

Rice, Richard. *The Openness of God*. Nashville: Review and Herald, 1980.

Roy, Steven. *How Much Does God Foreknow?* Downers Grove, IL: InterVarsity-Press, 2006.

Sanders, John. *The God Who Risks*. Downers Grove, IL: InterVarsity Press, 1998.

Ware, Bruce. "An Evangelical Reformulation of the Doctrine of the Immutability of God," *JETS* 29 (1986): 431–46.

War and Canaanite Genocide

Boettner, Loraine. *The Christian Attitude toward War*. Phillipsburg, NJ: Presbyterian and Reformed, 1940.

Clouse, Robert G. ed. *War: Four Christian Views*. Downers Grove, IL.: InterVarsity, 1981.

Craigie, Peter C. *The Problem of War in the Old Testament*. Grand Rapids: Eerdmans, 1978.

Cowles, C.S. "The Case for Radical Discontinuity," in *Show Them No Mercy: Four Views on God and Canaanite Genocide*. Grand Rapids: Zondervan, 2003, 13–44.

Fretheim, Terrence E. "God and Violence in the Old Testament," *Word and World* 24 (2004): 18–28.

Gundry, Stanley N. *Show Them No Mercy: Four Views on God and Canaanite Genocide*. Grand Rapids: Zondervan, 2003.

Hess, Richard S. and Elmer Martens, eds. *War in the Bible and Terrorism in the Twenty-First Century*. Winona Lake, IN: Eisenbrauns, 2008.

Holmes, Arthur F. *War and Christian Ethics*. Grand Rapids: Baker, 1975.

Long, V. Philips, "When God Declares War," *Christianity Today* 40 (October 28, 1996): 14–21.

Mendenhall, George E. "The Vengeance of Yahweh," in *The Tenth Generation*. Baltimore: Johns Hopkins University Press, 1973, 69–104.

Merrill, Eugene H. "The Case for Moderate Discontinuity," in *Show Them No Mercy: Four Views on God and Canaanite Genocide*. Grand Rapids: Zondervan, 2003, 63–94.

Miller, Patrick D., Jr. "God the Warrior: A Problem in Biblical Interpretation," *Interpretation* 19 (1965): 39–46.

Niehaus, Jeffrey J. "Joshua and Ancient Near Eastern Warfare," *Journal of the Evangelical Theological Society* 31 (1988): 37–50.

Younger, K. Lawson, Jr. "Ancient Conquest Accounts: A Study in Ancient Near Eastern and Biblical Historical Writing," in *Journal for the Study of the Old Testament* 98 Press, (1990).

Polygamy

Bruce, Willard. "Polygamy and the Church," *Concordia Theological Monthly.* 34 (1963): 223–32.

Dwight, S. E. *The Hebrew Wife*. New York: Leavitt, 1836.

Fountain, Oswald C. "Polygamy and the Church," *Missiology: An International Review* 11 (1963).

Gaskiyane, I. *Polygamy: As Cultural and Biblical Perspective*. Carlisle, UK: Piquant, 2000.

Holst, Robert, "Polygamy and the Bible," *International Review of Missions* 56 (1967): 205–13.

Parrinder, E. G. *The Bible and Polygamy.* London: SPCK, 1958.

Piper, Thomas S. "Did God Condone Polygamy?" *Good News Broadcaster* 35 (1977).

Satan and His Minions

Kluger, Rivkah Scharf. *Satan in the Old Testament.* Trans. Hildegard Nagel. Evanston, IL: Northwestern University Press, 1967.

Pagels, Elaine. *The Origin of Satan.* New York: Random House, 1995.

Women

Exum, J. Charyl, "The Ethics of Violence against Women,"in *The Bible in Ethics: The Second Sheffield Colloquium.* Eds. John W. Rogerson, Margaret Davies, and M. Daniel Carrol R. Journal for the Study of the Old Testament: Supplement Series 207, Sheffield, UK: Sheffield Academic, 1995, 248–271.

Freedman, R. David. "Women, a Power Equal to Man," *Biblical Archaeology Review* 9 (1983): 56–58

Gordon, Adoniram Judson, "The Ministry of Women," *Missionary Review of the World* VII, new series, December 1894.

Kaiser, Walter C. Jr. "Correcting Caricatures: The Biblical Teaching on Women," *Priscilla Papers* 19.2 (2005): 5–11.